God's Blueprint

By
Dr. Douglas Carr

Create Space: www.CreateSpace.com
Copyright 2014
Douglas Carr

Unless otherwise identified, Scripture quotations are from the HOLY BIBLE, NEW INTERNATIONAL VERSION, Copyright 1973, 1978, 1984 by International Bible Society. Used by permission of Zondervan Publishing House. All rights reserved.

Scripture quotations identified ASV are from the American Standard Version of the Bible.

Scripture quotations identified as KJV are from the King James Version of the Bible.

SCHEMATICS:
God's Blueprint versus Satan's Programming

ISBN-13: 978-1496176615   ISBN-10: 1496176618

Library of Congress Cataloging-in-Publication Data
Carr, Douglas,
    Schematics: God's Blueprint versus Satan's Programming.
    Summary: Comparing God's prophetic destiny to Satan's programming to hinder, defeat, or destroy Gods personal destiny in each person.
    This book is written to help people determine and come into agreement with the Lord's blueprint for their lives and to help them not be unaware of the devil's schemes to knock them off course. This book will assist the reader overcome Satan's programming to hinder or block their prophetic destiny.

    1. Deliverance. 2. Demonology. 3. Setting Captives Free. 4. Liberty--Religious aspects--Christianity. 5. Theology.

Books by Douglas Carr

Free Indeed! Deliverance Ministry

Beat Me Up Spirits

Free Indeed from Root Spirits

Schematics: God's Blueprint versus Satan's Programming

Getting to the Rotten Inner Core
(To be released soon)

All books available in print and Kindle
through **www.Amazon.com**
Look under Douglas Carr and find Titles.

Doug Carr Freedom Ministries
410 South Clay St.
Sturgis, Michigan 49091
www.dougcarrfreedomministries.com

Special Thanks!

There are several people who helped make this book possible. First is my dear wife Pamela who increasingly carries the load of the Church we pastor so I can concentrate on the writing the Lord has called me to.

Second is Beverly Bubb who has learned to navigate the Create Space system, making easy what seems impossible to me. Along with Bev is her son John Bubb who can figure out everything his mother is not able to.

Third is Christine McMillin who understands the intricacies of the updated word program I use. She has been able to figure out page numbering systems and fix the places where Word seems to take the writing out of this author's hands.

DOUGLAS CARR is known for his Free Indeed Seminars and for deep healing and deliverance ministries. His greatest calling is to equip the saints to set captives free.

Dr. Carr wants to help each city to have at least one church that is effective in deep healing and deliverance. There are people in every church and city that need more than salvation and discipleship alone. Many are caught in personal or ancestral sins, iniquities, curses and bondage issues that need deep level healing and deliverance.

Doug and his wife Pam have been ministering in the power of the Holy Spirit for deep healing and deliverance since the early 1990's. They have been teaching Free Indeed Seminars since 1995. They have five grown children, all of whom live within 15 miles of Doug and Pam's home in Sturgis, Michigan. God is so good!

Douglas Carr

CONTENTS:

Foreword 7
Introduction 9
1. The Tenure of Your Ways 10

Part I: Victory over Faces of Anger
2. Faces of Anger 22
3. The Face of Generational Anger 23
4. The Face of Un-yielded Expectations Anger 28
5. The Face of Erupting Anger 32
6. The Face of Selfish Anger 35
7. The Face of Learned Anger 37
8. The Face of Righteous Anger 40
9. It is Time to Break out of Prison! 43

Part II: Victory through Transformation
10. From Chaos to Calling 49
11. The Battle over Abundance 54
12. Treasures for Personal Transformation 58
13. Moving From Sin to Glory 68
14. Three Types of People 84
15. Power of the Holy Spirit for Right Living 91
16. In His SOVEREIGN Image 106

Part III: Victory through Spiritual Warfare
17. Parable of a Laptop With a Forgotten Cord 120
18. Overcoming Schematics and Obstacles to Healing 129
19. God's Blessings: Doing God's Will God's Way 143
20. Stumble thru' Da Clutter or Stand up & De-clutter? 146

Part IV: Victory through Obedience
21. Blessing or Curse—Centered on a Four Letter Word 158
22. O is Obey 162
23. B is Blessing 168
24. E is in Everything 172
25. Y is You 176
Conclusion 179

Foreword by Bill Sudduth

I have been ministering and teaching deliverance since my introduction to it during the Brownsville Revival in Pensacola, Florida; where I was a member of the pastoral care staff and head of the deliverance ministry. Doing deliverance is easy, but teaching people to walk in ongoing freedom can be very difficult. For example, we can cast out demons of anger and frustration, but even then the habits and roots of such behaviors often remain.

Ed Murphy, author of <u>The Handbook for Spiritual Warfare,</u> wrote that deliverance is about 45% pre-deliverance ministry, 10% deliverance and 45% post deliverance discipleship. Most deliverance ministers are so busy ministering deliverance that others need to come forward to help people work through Christian discipleship to address the root behaviors that gave the enemy permission to attack in the first place. Doug's book will help them do just that.

In <u>Schematics: God's Blueprint versus Satan's Programming</u>; Douglas explains how to recognize and win the battle that begins over each person's life before they are even born.

Too many people fail to understand that both God and Satan have a plan for their lives. Most Christians know that Jesus came that we might have life more abundantly. And many know that the devil comes to kill, steal and destroy. But the key player in this war really isn't God or the devil.

God has given each person his or her own sovereign will. God does have plans to prosper and not harm us. Satan does have plans to deceive and destroy. But God did not make people pawns -- He wants them to partner with Him for abundant life.

The reality is that Satan tries to make people do his bidding, but Believers can choose to resist him. <u>Schematics</u> explains that war in a way that is clear and precise. I quote from Doug's conclusion the prevailing key to victory: *"This is a choice that we all make intentionally or by default. God has given us personal sovereignty in the matter. Choose this day whom you will serve, for no man can serve two masters."* Schematics will help people make that choice and walk in ongoing victory.

I am pleased to recommend this new resource by Dr. Douglas Carr, a long standing member of the International Society of Deliverance Ministers over which I provide leadership and direction. Certainly it is a valuable new tool that will help many extend and secure the hard-fought for freedom of not only obtaining, but maintaining their victory over the schemes of the enemy.

Bill Sudduth
President
Righteous Acts Ministries, Inc.
International Society of Deliverance Ministers
Colorado Springs, CO
Phone: (850) 390-4104
E-mail: office@ramministry.org
Website: www.ramministry.org

Introduction

Somehow, we know there is a grand scheme of things for our lives and our world. But are we the grand master of this scheme, or its servant? Are we the puppeteer, or the puppet?

In life, sociology, and theology, the pendulum often swings to extremes. On the one side, people just give in and let stuff happen--victims of what they assume to be some overriding scheme for their lives. On the other extreme, they act as if they are the sole masters of their own destinies, as if no one else, not even God, has a say in their lives. Neither extreme is good, healthy, or correct.

Religion actually helps muddy the waters. The extreme view of God's sovereignty that attributes everything--good or bad, to God's irrevocable will, makes Him the author of all pain and suffering. This view ultimately holds God responsible for famine, sickness, murder, and every other source of pain and suffering. On the other hand, deism says that God set the universe in motion, but does not interfere with how it runs. In other words, God simply left our lives and world in human hands for better or for worse.

The truth is far more liberating, and knowing it will set us free. Both God and Satan have a scheme for every life, and God has granted people personal sovereignty to choose whom they will serve.

As a deliverance minister I offer this book to help people realize that they can choose to follow God's blueprint for their lives while purposely rejecting Satan's programming.

Chapter 1
The Tenure of Your Ways

Children are asked what they want to be when they grow up. I wanted to be a lion tamer and work for a circus. Later, God called me into the ministry. So, I guess I got what I wanted! At times it feels like I work for a circus--only the Lion is taming me!

The Bible mentions two lions that we will focus on here. One is Jesus, who is the Lion of the tribe of Judah; and the other is Satan, who is called a prowling lion who is seeking whom he may devour.

These words of Jesus are familiar:

> "The thief cometh not, but for to steal, and to kill, and to destroy: I am come that they might have life, and that they might have it more abundantly." John 10:10 KJV.

It is time to look deeper at this verse, because it reveals that both God and Satan have a "schematic" for each life: one leads to abundance and the other to loss.

God's schematic leads to the abundant life, which comes from being whom God specifically created each one of us to be. When we truly become who we are supposed to be -- life becomes abundant!

This is true in my own life. Even though preaching and teaching were the last things I thought I wanted to do, they became what I most like to do, because God created me to be a preacher, a teacher, and a deliverance minister.

I made a lot of money when I worked as a home supervisor, serving people with severe developmental disabilities. That was the easiest job of my life and I enjoyed it, but my life wasn't abundant--because that wasn't God's grand scheme for me.   No one can know true abundance apart from being who God created them to BE, so they can DO what He created them to DO.

The thief tries to steal, kill and destroy God's tenor for our lives. He uses anything he can to convince us that we cannot be who we were created to be. If that doesn't work, he discourages us from doing what God prepared, in advance, for us to do. The devil tries to make us think that failure is final, or that we can't get to where we are going, from where we are.

I was a late bloomer in the things of God. I wasn't born again until age twenty-one, or called to prepare for ministry until four years after I graduated from high school. By then, I was already a husband and a father, struggling to make ends meet.

Satan tried to convince me that I didn't have enough brains or money to go to college. He did the same thing 22 years later, when I sensed the call to graduate work at Wagner Leadership Institute. I am thankful for a lesson that I learned from a Psychology Professor at Spring Arbor College after I had reacted poorly to the scoring of a vocational analysis test. Rather than affirm my calling to minister, the test revealed that I was best suited to be a mortician. I knew God's will for my life, and that wasn't it. I can still see what he scratched on my paper, "God's call=God's enabling."

But, Satan also has a goal and plan for each life. He loves to trick us, and will even use religion to do so.

The apostle Paul was created to impact the world with the Gospel and with his epistles, but was diverted from this for years as a religious Pharisee that hated Christians and the Gospel message. The devil tricks some with the lure of riches.

Christian parents may be so caught up in trying to give their children the best the world has to offer, that they forget to offer themselves to God for their children.

Wanna-be preachers are told, "If God calls you to be a preacher, don't stoop to be a king." But truth also says, "If God calls you to be a king, don't stoop to be a preacher."

Some people choose to be preachers when they are not chosen by the Lord to be preachers. They kick against the goads and make themselves, and those who listen, miserable.

In his attempt to kill, steal, and destroy the devil lures people to try to be someone they are not meant to be. God, on the other hand, wants to help people become whom He created them to be, for that is the essence of abundant life. God's greatest desire for his children is to guide them in the tenor of their ways. Tenor refers to God's grand scheme for a person's life.

The abundant life that Jesus referred to is linked to God's tenor for our lives! Too many fail to understand the true meaning of Proverbs 22:6. So many preachers and parents think that if they make children read their Bibles, pray, and go to church when they are young, that when they are old they will not turn from it. But those same parents and preachers end up lamenting that many children grew up and left the church.

A 2002 Southern Baptists Youth survey states that 88% of youth will leave the church. Life Way Research of 2007 states that 70% of youth leave the church, and only 35% eventually return. An Assembly of God link records that 66% of youth leave the Church, and Barna records 61% leaving the church. He states: "'Most twenty-something's' place their Christianity on the shelf."

Cross Examined.Org states that 70-75% of youth leave the church. Part of the problem is that parents, preachers, and teachers try to make children be what they want them to be, rather than finding out what God created them to be. This happened to me. My parents started dragging me to church when I was in sixth grade. I liked the singing but was soon asked to be an altar boy.

I wasn't cut out to carry a cross on a stick and look serious all the time. The priest and my parents wanted me to be an altar boy, but that was not who God created me to be. Had I continued in the plans they had for me, I might still be in a church that is far different than the kind of church God wanted me to pastor.

God's will is more about BEING, than it is about DOING. God, who formed us in the womb, and knew us before we were born, knows exactly whom He created each one of us to be. Therefore, as we fully surrender to the Lord, we become whom we were created to be, and abundant life follows! That may sound simple, but God's schematics for each of our lives are only discovered as we tear down the enemy's schemes and grow in God's plan for our lives.

It is not easy to become whom God created us to be, but that is the only way to press into abundant life. We may go through many trials doing our own thing, or trying to be whom somebody else wants us to be. But, IF we surrender to the Lord wherever we happen to be, He is strong enough to bring us all the way in to his blueprint--no matter how old we are!

Joseph faced some pretty tough circumstances but he was destined to become the second highest-in-command in Egypt and to save Israel from famine. He later said, "Satan meant it for evil, but God meant it for good."

Moses lost all self-confidence, and tried to get out of God's assignment before surrendering to God's call in front of a burning bush. God asked him some burning questions, like, "Who made your mouth? Who gives you the power to speak? What is that in your hand?" When Moses finally surrendered, he became the mighty deliverer God created him to be.

Daniel was kidnapped, taken into a strange land, stripped of his identity, and given a pagan name. He faced danger in the lion's den, but he kept on praying and seeking God three times a day; and God exalted him to be the wise man and chief-adviser to the King according to His blueprint for Daniel's life.

Esther was orphaned at an early age. She was adopted by her Uncle Mordecai and submitted to his direction. She was put on display before a pagan king who had a different woman paraded before him and made available for his pleasure each night. She faced huge obstacles but never lost hope that God had something better in store for her. God's grand scheme for her life was for her to become the queen who would save Israel from annihilation.

Paul was groomed to be a great Pharisee. His parents, teachers and peers had a plan for him to be a leader of the Pharisees within Judaism. But that was not who God created him to be. Paul was so intent at kicking against the goads of God's plan for his life that God had to knock him to the ground to awaken him to the reality that He created him to be an apostle to the Gentiles.

Self-confident Peter thought he was in control of his own life. He was a self-made man and thought nothing could get in the way of his personal goals. God took him down a few pegs after he denied Jesus. It was after he totally messed up that he was finally able to surrender the reins, and allow God to shape him according to His preordained schematic: to be the mighty Christian evangelist and apostle that God created him to be.

Just like these heroes, we may have our own plan for our lives. Or, perhaps we have given into the plan a parent, boss, or spouse has for our lives. It's easy to lose track of our way, especially when things aren't going our way. But God! God has a way of making all things work together for the good of those who love him and are truly committed to him.

It's also easy for us to misunderstand God's way for our children--especially if we let our hopes trump God's plans for them. God wants parents to help their children discover His tenor for their lives. But Satan wants parents to make their children miss God's schematics so they will fall short of His glory for their lives.

Proverbs 22:6 is often misused and misunderstood, because of the way it is usually quoted and applied.

> Train up a child in the way he should go: and when he is old, he will not depart from it. Proverbs 22:6 KJV.

Parents and preachers often take this to mean that they should train up children in the way THEY think they should go. That is NOT the intent of this passage. The true intent which is clearly seen if you look at the Hebrew word is best translated "in the tenor of his way." Unfortunately this verse usually is mistranslated or misunderstood as "the way he should go," which many parents and leaders further pervert by thinking it says "in the way I want the child to go."

In fairness to the KJV, it adds the following footnote in some Bibles: "Train...: or, Catechize, {Heb. <u>in his way</u>} (<u>in the child's particular way</u>)" These helpful footnotes make reference to "the tenor of his way." That tenor reveals that each person is uniquely ASSIGNED & DESIGNED by God.

The child's tenor is God's inbred schematic, to lead to abundant living.

Other Bible translations release further insight:
- Train up a child in the way he should go *[and in keeping with his individual gift or bent]*, and when he is old he will not depart from it. Proverbs 22:6 AMP.
- Teach children *in a way that fits their needs,* and even when they are old, they will not leave the right path. Proverbs 22:6 LEB.
- Train the child concerning his way; even when he is old, he will not stray from it. (Footnotes: Literally "on the mouth of his way") Proverbs 22:6 Easy to Read.

The best translation that I've found is Darby's:
- Train up the child according to the tenor of his way, and when he is old he will not depart from it." Proverbs 22:6 Darby.

The English Thesaurus lists these words under *tenor*: mood, tone, gist, drift, meaning, sense, theme, intention, tendency and purpose. One dictionary describes it as: "*uninterrupted course*, the drift of something spoken or written, the concept, object or person meant in a metaphor, a continuance in a course, movement, or activity." Another adds "the flow or meaning in something."

Bringing up a child--whether a young child or God's adult child--according to the tenor of his or her way, means "training them to be everything God created them to be."

If God created them to be a banker, then we would kick against the goads trying to make them preachers. If God created them to be musicians, we would resist God's purposes if we try to turn them into soccer players.

Christian thinking has given into the error of false dualism that says some things are sacred and other things are secular. We have wrongly thought that playing music in church is sacred, but playing music in school is secular. We have considered the call to preach as sacred, but the call to be a public school teacher or work in a factory, as secular. That may be the world's thinking, but it isn't God's. The Bible teaches us that we are to do everything that we do, for the Lord--and that makes everything sacred!

> Whatever you do, work at it with all your heart, as working for the Lord, not for men, since you know that you will receive an inheritance from the Lord as a reward. It is the Lord Christ you are serving. Colossians 3:23-24.

> So whether you eat or drink or whatever you do, do it all for the glory of God. I Corinthians 10:31.

Discovering God's tenure for each child is paramount to helping them to be everything God created them to be. Failure to follow God's schematic for a child opens the way for Satan's schematic by default. Nothing in parenting is more critical than partnering with God's plan for the child. This is far too important to leave to chance.

Parents, teachers and children's and youth workers should first ask God about His tenure for each child. Then they need to listen until He answers.

It is a terrible mistake to think that prayer is a one-way street! God wants to reveal each child's tenure and He will if we ask, seek, knock, and listen.

We should ask children and adults what they think they are supposed to be. Simply asking what their interests are is a great start. It is as we get to know the child through God's eyes; we will discover what God put into the child.

If we look closely we can help them develop according to God's individual design for each one. Part of this includes finding out what they really like to do, and helping them do that.

Young and innocent children haven't learned how to mask their desires like most adults do. What they do tends to flow from who they are. A musical child will sing and play instruments. An athletic child will play sports and the like. As we grow older we become concerned about the expectations of others so our doing becomes performance-based rather than flowing from personal desire and destiny.

Many parents and children are so caught up in texting, Facebook, E-mails and cell phones that no time is left for real conversation between them and their children. That is part of Satan's scheme to keep children from being brought up according to the tenor of their ways.

If parents don't have enough courtesy and respect for their children to turn off their own phones during meal times, it is time that they learn it. And if parents don't have the intestinal fortitude to make their children turn off their phones, iPod's and TV's during meal times and family prayer times, may God release a new supply of conviction! How can parents know their children if they are distracted by their technology and media? And how can they discover the tenor of a child's way if the child is so addicted to screens, small and large, that he can't look into the parent's eyes while talking?

It is critical that parents discover God's blueprint for their children. It is just as important that we seek out His schematic for our own lives. How can we discover who God created us to be?

First, we need to ask Holy Spirit and listen, until we have some answers. Who better knows the blueprint for a life than the One who created it?

God created each person with a specific tenure. We enter abundant life as we discover and yield to God's schematic for our personal lives.

Married people can ask their spouse how they see God's schematic for their life. My wife knows me better than I know myself. She sees my blind self--the part of me that others see but that I cannot see myself. For instance, she brought to my attention that it looks like I am frowning when I am really concentrating on what others are saying, and that makes it look like I disapprove of what they are saying.

People, whose parents are living, can ask them what they sense God created them to be, even if they are not saved. God loves to use parents to bring young and adult children into their destinies. I asked my father to write me such a note years ago. He gave great wisdom, insight and affirmation even though he wasn't nearly as close to the Lord as he came to be in his later years.

Ask God to help you see yourself through His eyes. Part of the devil's schematics is tempting us to view ourselves as less than we are or more highly than we should. He tempts us with self-rejection, inferiority and the like, or with pride. But, when we can see ourselves through God's eyes, we gain confidence without pride.

Reflect on what you most enjoy doing. Religion says that God wants to make us do what we most hate to do. True intimate friendship (see John 15:15) with God knows that God wants to lead us into fullness by helping us be everything we are. Religion makes us fear that full commitment might lead to eating bugs on a mission field. But true relationship leads us to the fullness of whom we are and that leads to abundant life

While striving to define God's schematic for your life, it is helpful to serve in various capacities until one really clicks.

God created us on purpose, for a purpose and as we find His purpose for our lives, we finally sense we are doing what we were made to do. In the church world, it is great to serve in various capacities until you find the one where you have maximum effectiveness and minimum weariness.

Give yourself permission to fail. We are human and we all make mistakes. Failure is not final. With God's help, we can learn to "fail forward" and use past mistakes as stepping stones to future glory.

Finally, the best approach to finding God's will is to discover who He says you are. At the end of your life you don't want to sing "I did it my way." Life will be abundant on earth and in heaven when we become who God created us to be. Then we can do what we do HIS way -- the way He prepared in advance for us to do. Becoming who you are is not narcissistic, when you focus on who God created you to be.

"To thine own self be true," is selfish independence, but to be true to God's design for you is the greatest act of submission possible. I close this chapter with Ephesians 4:7-13 from The Message Bible, with emphasis mine:

> But that doesn't mean you should all look and speak and act the same. Out of the generosity of Christ, each of us is given his own gift. The text for this is,
> He climbed the high mountain,
> He captured the enemy and seized the booty,
> He handed it all out in gifts to the people.

Is it not true that the One who climbed up also climbed down, down to the valley of earth? And the One who climbed down is the One who climbed back up, up to highest heaven. He handed out gifts above and below, filled heaven with his gifts, filled earth with his gifts. He handed out gifts of apostle, prophet, evangelist, and pastor-teacher *to train Christ's followers in skilled servant work*, working within Christ's body, the church, *until we're all moving rhythmically and easily with each other, efficient and graceful in response to God's Son, fully mature adults, fully developed within and without,* fully alive like Christ.

No prolonged infancies among us, please. We'll not tolerate babes in the woods, small children who are an easy mark for impostors. God wants us to grow up, to know the whole truth and tell it in love—like Christ in everything. We take our lead from Christ, who is the source of everything we do. He keeps us in step with each other. His very breath and blood flow through us, nourishing us so that we will grow up healthy in God, robust in love. Ephesians 4:7-13 MSG.

God does have a blueprint and tenor for each life but Satan also has his programming at work in our lives to keep us from recognizing God's call and plan for our lives. We will look at that next.

Chapter 2
Faces of Anger

I was driving home from a series of deliverance appointments at Community Healing Rooms in Novi, Michigan and listening to a message by Prophet Ed Watts, when suddenly I sensed the Lord saying, "You need to write on the topic of "The Faces of Anger." Later in my Daily Listening Room, the Lord led me to list six faces of anger:

1) The Face of Generational Anger.
2) The Face of Un-Yielded Expectations Anger.
3) The Face of Erupting Anger.
4) The Face of Selfish Anger.
5) The Face of Learned Anger.
6) The Face of Righteous Anger.

Each one of these faces of anger can have demons attached. We have little mastery over the demonic component until we master the human components. In the following chapters we will look at each of them.

Chapter 3
The Face of Generational Anger

Anger can be passed down through: generational lines; by example; through vows and curses; through inner vows; and/or through demons.

Consider how Satan's programming works through generational examples of anger. Children of angry parents tend to become angry adults. If children see a parent fingering people when they are angry, they will go and do likewise. If they hear their parents yelling at each other, they will tend to follow that example in their own marriages. Satan uses such things to create his dastardly schematic for a child. People need to take definitive steps to break free of the devil's schemes, in order to follow the Lord into His freedom and plan.

The first step of action is to forgive parents for their anger. The fact that parents were angry, and hurt their children through their anger, does not negate the need to forgive. You can be right about your parents being wrong, but you must still choose to forgive. This can be done in the privacy of your own prayer time. Just choose to forgive and tell God, "I choose to forgive my parents for their anger, and its affect on my life."

The second step of action is to seek deep healing from that anger. Some can just ask Jesus to reveal where He was and what He was doing when they were hurt by someone's anger. Others may need the help of deep-healing ministry to do this. They know they need to forgive, but may need some help forming the words and working through forgiveness. If unforgiveness is long-lived, especially if it remains from childhood, the person may need help discerning and casting down demons.

Generational Vows or Curses of Anger

Satan works his schematics through ancestral means whenever he can. Unless people descend from a long line of victorious Christians, they inherit generational vows and curses.

Generational vows--especially those from secret societies like the Freemasons and Eastern Star—are strong. Satan uses the power of vows, curses, and iniquitous patterns- knowing they are passed down at least four generations. The Freemason Lodge is a powerful form of witchcraft, even though it looks good on the outside.

My hometown put an old Shriners' fire truck on display during the summer of 2012. My prayer partner and I prayed over the place that was set apart for that truck. The Shriners' arm of Freemasonry practices benevolence, but it is the beautiful side of evil. The vows of Masonry release all sorts of curses upon people and their descendants, including physical, emotional, financial, and the like.

Doing a Masonic Release Prayer is a crucial step to break Satan's schematic working through these ancestral vows. The Masonic Release Prayers that I recommend come from Selwyn Steven's website, www.jubileeresources.org and may be used for free. Just click the prayer tab, and look for prayers of release from Freemasonry.

Another scheme of Satan comes through curses of anger which must be broken. A curse of anger may be as simple as, "When you grow up, I hope you will have children that act just the way you are acting." If anger is a part of that behavior, then a curse of anger has been released. When a mom says, "You are just like your Dad," or a father says, "You are just like your Mom," the power of death may be in their tongue. If the dad or mother was an angry person, the child was just cursed to carry on that anger.

It is not enough to just forgive parents for such curses. The curse needs to be confessed and renounced, until the generational stronghold is broken.

Inner vows are made by children and quickly forgotten. For example, if a child judges a parent's anger and says, "I will never get mad at my children like my mom (or dad) gets mad at me," the power of what they said becomes an inner vow. Such inner vows are quickly forgotten, but the power is there until they are broken. These inner vows have greater power because they are hidden, and become like computer programs that respond through the very anger that the child so hated in the parent.

I compare inner vows to hearing a song on the radio that you don't like. You immediately change the channel, but later find yourself humming the very tune that you don't like. That is how inner vows work. Parents catch themselves treating their own children or spouses, the way they vowed as children they would never do.

Another illustration of inner vows is the way viruses attack computers. They find their way in unawares and wait for the opportunity to shut the whole program down.

Five Steps to Victory over Inner Vows:
Step 1: Ask the Holy Spirit to reveal inner vows.

Confessing and renouncing inner vows is pivotal in breaking free of Satan's schematics.

The first step in breaking inner vows is asking Holy Spirit to reveal them. This often takes place during deep healing ministry, but God will reveal such vows to anyone who seeks His voice on the matter.

Step 2: Forgiving those who hurt you.

The devil has legal access to our lives through bitterness. (Ephesians 4:26-27) Miracles are often released when people intentionally forgive others for the pain they caused them.

Step 3: Confessing inner vows.

The third step in breaking inner vows, is confessing the vows you made. For example, if God reveals that you have made an inner vow to never treat your children the way your parents treated you, choose to forgive your parents and confess to God that you made the inner vow. Once you have done that, you can renounce it and break it, in the name of the Lord Jesus Christ!

Step 5: Renouncing inner vows.

Confession leads to God's forgiveness. Renouncing leads to Satan's release. Once forgiveness is received it is important to simply say "In Jesus' Name I renounce the inner vows of . . ."

Step 6: Deliverance.

A final step in breaking inner vows is deliverance.

If you are comfortable working self-deliverance, just ask God to reveal which demons have attached themselves through your inner vows. Once He has answered your prayer, you can simply ask God to remove them from your life, or cast them out yourself. Those who are not familiar or comfortable with self-deliverance should seek the help of a deliverance minister.

Generational Demons of Anger

Un-repented sin always gives the devil a stronghold. Ephesians 4:27-29 indicates that demons have a literal foothold in the lives of those who hang onto long-held anger. These demons often follow family lines. Familiar spirits may attach to family members after a death in the family. Demons do not remain with dead people. They seek a living host, and often look first within the closest flesh and blood members of the family. Sometimes they are confirmed through the laying on of hand or other touching of someone who is deceased.

Recognizing and casting out family demons is crucial. If you see a negative family characteristic flowing from generation to generation, there may be a familiar spirit attached to keep descendants in bondage to Satan's programming.

It is important to confess one's own negative thoughts, words and actions. If you have agreed with or flowed with sinful family traits, it is time to disagree! Confess and renounce the sin and behavior, break down and demolish those generational strongholds and cast out the corresponding demons.

Chapter 4
The Face of Un-yielded Expectations Anger

People may become angry when they feel their personal rights are being violated. For example, if a man feels he has the right to be intimate with his wife twice a week, he will become angry if that happens only once a week.

Anger is often a symptom of un-yielded expectations. People disappoint us. If we expect them to always please, we will be angry when they don't.

A story is told about a man who started blessing his neighbors with $5.00 every day. The people were thrilled at first. They knew they hadn't earned that $5.00 and they didn't expect it. The man continued giving them $5.00 a day, for several weeks. Suddenly, he stopped giving them $5.00 a day. Can you guess what happened? The people were mad at him. They wondered what happened to the $5.00 a day they had received. Now they were expecting that money, and became angry when they didn't get it.

Two Steps to tear un-yielded expectations anger down:

A vital step to tearing this anger down is recognizing anger as a signpost of un-yielded expectations. When you are angry, ask God what perceived personal right is being violated.

The day before I wrote this, I attempted to activate software I had purchased along with a new computer. I called the toll-free help-line at 9:30 a.m. and was transferred several times from one department to another. Thank God, I never became aggressive, but I did become assertive after 90 minutes of being put on hold and being transferred time after time.

The final time I was transferred I said, "Listen, I have been transferred and put on hold several times already and have wasted an hour and half without any resolution of my problem. You either need you to stick with me until this problem is resolved or transfer me to customer service, so I can return my computer and purchase one locally where I can receive help in a timely manner."

Thankfully, I didn't get angry because I had already asked the Lord, "Why is this getting to me?" while I was on hold. He told me that my impatience and frustration was not spiritual, but carnal. So I confessed it, renounced it and commanded any demons that came in, to leave in Jesus' name. I coughed violently a few times, and was able to be assertive, apart from anger.

It took the final technician over an hour to figure out that the problem was in the software server, but he stayed with it until the program was downloaded and working properly. I later sent an e-mail commending the technician by name, and recommending him for a promotion and a raise.

The second step in dealing with un-yielded expectations anger is yielding your personal rights and expectations to the Lord. I had to yield my personal expectation to having my computer issue solved in a timely manner to the Lord. Had I not done that I would have carried that anger throughout that day.

King David was a man after God's own heart. He experienced all sorts of dire circumstances and calamities, but he remained faithful, because his hopes and expectations were in the Lord. A secret to his favor in God's eyes is seen below.

> "My soul finds rest in God alone; my salvation comes from him. He alone is my rock and my salvation; he is my fortress, I will never be shaken. ...Find rest, O my soul, in God alone; my hope comes from him." Psalm 62:1-2, 5.

This is huge! People will let you down--no matter how much they love you or you love them. Spouses can be inconsiderate. Parents and children can get so caught up in their own stuff, that they can't see the needs of others. If we put our hope and expectations in them, they will let us down and anger will follow. But if we truly yield our rights to the Lord, He will never let us down.

Some of David's thoughts from Psalm 130 jumped out at me a few months ago. My wife had worked the voting polls from 6 a.m. - 10:40 p.m. the day before, and I didn't see her note asking me to wake her up. So, I began devotions alone, hoping she would get some extra sleep since I had to be at the church at 6:00 a.m. These words flashed brightly before me as I read them.

> Out of the depths I cry to You, O LORD; O Lord, hear my voice. Let Your ears be attentive to my cry for mercy. *If you, O LORD, kept a record of sins, O Lord, who could stand?* But with You there is forgiveness; therefore You are feared. *I wait for the LORD, my soul waits, and in His word I put my hope. My soul waits for the Lord more than watchmen wait for the morning,* more than watchmen wait for the morning. *O Israel put your hope in the LORD, for with the LORD is unfailing love and with Him is full redemption.* He himself will redeem Israel from all their sins.
> Psalm 130. (emphasis mine)

How did David rise to greatness in the midst of all his enemies? How did he keep on keeping on, when people laid in wait to destroy him? He gave it all to God and kept on going with God -- refusing to let anger destroy him because of unfulfilled expectations.

I finally noticed my wife's note to wake her up just as I was leaving the house. I hurried back and woke her up and explained I had not seen her note. Always a step ahead of me in learning life's lessons she merely said "Must be God wanted me to sleep a little longer -- now I need to get moving." Praise God, her expectations were already yielded!

Chapter 5
The Face of Erupting Anger
Which Bubbles under the Surface until it Erupts

Erupting anger bubbles under the surface like a volcano. It is usually lodged in deep inner wounds that have never been fully addressed.

There are times when people blow up and have no clue why they are so angry. The anger is far greater than the present situation calls for. This is often true in marriage, especially if it is a second marriage, or if one or both partners had an abusive childhood. They get so angry that it takes them by surprise and are baffled by that level of anger.

Such anger may linger from unresolved issues from childhood or previous relationships. The partner does something that subconsciously recalls similar emotions or hurts from the past and the person reacts not only to what is presently done, but also to things done previously by others.

For example, if your father embarrassed you and made an example of you and your mate does something similar, your anger may blow with double force. Or if you had a parent who was controlling and manipulative then unresolved anger from that may erupt when someone else tries to manipulate or control you. Paul says that ongoing anger gives the devil a literal place to stand in our lives:

> "In your anger do not sin": Do not let the sun go down while you are still angry, and do not give the devil a foothold. Ephesians 4:26-27.

If you have unresolved anger from past abuse that anger may be released toward others who do something similar.

Four Steps to Freedom:

1. Ask God to reveal it.

The first step in resolving erupting anger is asking the Lord to reveal the root of that anger. Simply make confession when your anger is stronger than it should be in a given situation. Then ask the Lord to reveal the deeper root of that anger. When God reveals the root of your current anger, you can remove the root of bitterness that defiles you and stop producing the fruit of anger from that root.

2. Forgive.

The second step in resolving the anger that erupts is to forgive those who hurt you in that way. Begin with the ones who hurt you first and work through the list, until the foothold of bitterness is destroyed.

3. Renounce.

After you confess your anger make sure you renounce it and its hold on you. Once that is complete you can ask God to remove any demons that gained entrance through your anger and bitterness.

4. Seek healing for your brokenness.

Ask Jesus to heal your broken heart. When Jesus announced his purpose in Luke 4:18-19, He said He was anointed to heal fragmented hearts. People who have been deeply wounded may have their hearts splintered to the point that they have what is now called D.I.D. (Dissociative Identity Disorder) James speaks of it as double-mindedness. (literally "two- (or several) -souled") It is common for deliverance ministers to refer to such brokenness as fragmentation.

Jesus is anointed to draw all the broken pieces of your heart back together and make you whole.

As Dr. Charles Kraft teaches so well, deep wounds require deep healing and such healing is available to those who seek the Lord privately, or through deep healing ministry.

Chapter 6
The Face of Selfish Anger

"America's Funniest Videos" showed a clip of a young boy who was throwing a temper tantrum. His mother chose to ignore him and went to a different room. Time and again that boy moved to a new place so his mother could see him throwing his fit. It was quite funny--but such selfish anger becomes tragic if left unchecked.

Many people seem to think that the world revolves around them. They want what they want, how they want it and when they want it. We've all heard selfish or self-righteous people blow up at helpless store clerks or waitresses. Unfortunately, such anger is also displayed within marriages, families, work places and even churches.

I remember such anger in a man who was on a church board years before I learned how to handle such things. There were two older women on the same board who wanted to step down because this man kept spouting off to anyone who disagreed with him. For the sake of the older saints I finally stood up to the man. As he began his usual tirade I told him to sit down and be quiet until he could discuss the matter at hand calmly. Refusing to have his selfish anger corrected he pulled his wife out of our church and went on a search to find one where his anger wouldn't be checked.

Satan's schematics working through that man purposed to destroy all those around him. After he died his wife came for ministry and I discovered he had been abusive to his wife. His anger stopped the progress of church meetings and held his wife and children in bondage.

Three Steps to Victory:
1. Grow up and wise up.

Selfish and manipulative anger is of the devil, not of God. Getting angry because others don't see things your way divides and destroys. It really isn't all about you. There are other people all around you that are just as important and have as many feelings as you do.

The man who left my church was as childish and selfish as the boy in the AFV video that kept moving so his mother could see his tantrum.

Think of the places you've seen selfish anger at work: in lines at a store, while traveling busy highways, with people at work, with young children and childish adults. Man's anger does not work the righteousness of God. It is a schematic of the devil, to detour people and organizations from God's plan.

Paul said,

> "When I was a child, I talked like a child, I thought like a child, I reasoned like a child. When I became a man, I put childish ways behind me." 1 Corinthians 13:1.

2. Confess and renounce selfish anger.

There comes a time when we need to come to grips with selfish anger, and repent. True repentance is a change of heart that leads to a change of behavior. Ask God to change your heart and deliver you from selfish anger.

3. Seek deliverance.

Step three is to seek deliverance from spirits of anger, because ongoing anger always gives demons a foothold.

Chapter 7
The Face of Learned Anger

People from angry homes learn improper ways of dealing with disappointments. They may have seen their parents yell and scream at each other or take out their anger on them. Children from such environments may think that angry ways are normal.

Angry ways are not normal—not for cross-bought, blood-washed, Spirit-filled Believers! Unresolved anger is SIN. Treating others poorly, because you are angry, is wrong. Children are programmed to think that their parents are always right. So, if the parents are angry, the children believe anger is a normal response.

It is amazing to witness people as they discover that not everything their parents said and did was right. I've seen senior citizens come to the light, when the Holy Spirit reveals that the mean or angry things their parents did were not right and contrary to God's will.

Six Steps to Freedom:
1. Ask God to show you the truth.

Step one in resolving learned anger is asking God to reveal truth. It is important to respond quickly to conviction from Holy Spirit. Light received, brings more light. Light rejected, brings darkness. So, when Holy Spirit brings things to light, we need to quickly confess where we are wrong, and ask Him to lead us into truth.

2. Forgive those who were angry with you.

It is hard to receive forgiveness for things you haven't forgiven others for. If you have lived among angry people, you have probably been the target of their anger. Forgive those who were angry with you, and ask God to heal your heart of the damage it caused.

3. Confess sinful anger to the Lord.

If we confess our sins, he is faithful and just and will forgive us our sins and purify us from all unrighteousness. 1 John 1:9.

Ephesians 4:26 begins with "Be ye angry and sin not". It is not a sin to be angry but it is sin to let your anger linger. So step one is confess to the Lord the *sins* that flow from anger.

4. Confess iniquitous patterns of anger.

God forgives sins when we confess them but iniquities are deeper than sins.

Iniquities are the twisting, distortion or bent within the character that sin springs from. God's way of dealing with generational or personal iniquities and faults is to confess them to godly leaders and ask them to pray that you be healed. (See James 5:12-16)

5. Ask God to show you people who aren't angry.

Ask God to point out role models who are not angry. God will use their lack of anger to inspire you and teach you that there are better ways of dealing with things that seem to be out of control.

6. Seek deliverance.

Finally, deliverance is usually needed to break free of learned anger. Demons take advantage of such cracks in our spiritual armor. Demons of anger, generational anger, frustration and the like must be cast out, either by a deliverance ministry or self-deliverance.

Chapter 8
The Face of Righteous Anger

When I was first saved I heard talk about "righteous indignation." It was taught that some anger is wrong but righteous indignation meant getting mad about the things God gets mad about. The working understanding of righteous indignation appeared to be "If you are mad -- that is sinful anger, but if I am mad -- it is righteous indignation." (Yeah, right!)

There is such a thing as righteous indignation. I looked up the words "anger and God" and found them together in forty-two verses: God's anger was in two other verses, "Lord and anger" appeared in one hundred three verses, "Lord and angry" in forty verses, "God and angry" in nineteen additional verses. "Wrath" is found in one hundred ninety verses. There are times that Jesus showed righteous indignation.

There were two times when he drove the money changers out of the temple. Jesus was angry enough to drive people out of the temple with whips—a one-man Rambo with such fierce anger in his countenance that one man put dozens to flight. He also said things to his disciples like "Are you still so dull?" and "Why couldn't you stay awake with me one hour?" But Jesus never sinned. His secret? Jesus was angry only at the things the Father was angry about it. His anger was not about self. It was about the Kingdom of God.

There are many issues that God is angry about: abortion, sexual sin, perversion, injustice, ignoring the needs of the poor, etc. But righteous anger is fully surrendered to the Lord!

God may be angry with elective abortion but he does not want crusaders to bomb abortion clinics.

God may be angry with perverted life styles but he doesn't want vigilantes to drive their hummers into Gay Pride parades. God is angry with false religions but he doesn't want men to march into temples and start shooting. Truly righteous anger is fully under Holy Spirit control! James sums this up in the following passage:

> My dear brothers, take note of this: Everyone should be quick to listen, slow to speak and slow to become angry, for man's anger does not bring about the righteous life that God desires. Therefore, get rid of all moral filth and the evil that is so prevalent and humbly accept the word planted in you, which can save you. Do not merely listen to the word, and so deceive yourselves. Do what it says.
> James 1:19-22.

In previous chapters we looked at six faces of anger:
1) The Face of Generational Anger
2) The Face of Un-Yielded Expectations Anger
3) The Face of Erupting Anger
4) The Face of Selfish Anger
5) The Face of Learned Anger and
6) The Face of Righteous Anger.

James says it isn't enough to hear what God says about anger. We need to be doers of the Word and not hearers only. Each face of anger may have demons attached. James compares anger to moral filth and tells us to humbly accept this word which can save us--from ANGER!

Paul wrote:

> Be ye angry, and sin not: let not the sun go down upon your wrath: Neither give place to the devil.
> Ephesians 4:26-27 KJV.

We need to own up if we have an anger problem.

I call you to deal with that problem and to apply what God is revealing about the faces of anger. Don't give up and don't let up until your anger is fully dealt with! If you need deep healing, get it. If you need counseling, get it. Do not let anger rob you of everything God has in store for you and those you love.

Chapter 9
It is time to break out of prison!

Matthew Eighteen is a marvelous chapter concerning preservation and restoration. Our focus will be on the latter part of the chapter but I want to give a brief overview of the rest of the chapter in order set it within its proper context of protecting and restoring.

Matthew 18:1-4 focuses on childlike humility. Jesus tells us that we need to change and become like little children in order to enter the kingdom. He points to a child and says that whoever humbles himself like that child is greatest in the Kingdom of heaven.

Children recognize their need for help from someone bigger than they are. They are dependent upon others to help them do what they cannot do for themselves. Childlike humility is part of God's schematic for us just like pride is part of Satan's schematic. Children are also amazingly quick to forgive when asked for forgiveness.

Matthew 18:5-11 focuses on protecting children. Jesus instructs people to welcome little children like they would Him, and warns that if they cause one of the little ones to sin that it would be better for them to have a large millstone hung around their neck and be cast into the depths of the sea.

He makes it very clear that any offense against a child is an offense toward God and has eternal consequences. As a deliverance minister I sit on the opposite side of the desk from victims and perpetrators. Victims usually need deep healing for their pain plus deliverance from demons that took advantage of it. Perpetrators usually were victims before they became perpetrators. Both need healing from offenses done against them but perpetrators also have to address their offenses toward God by offending others, especially children.

Matthew 18:12-14 concentrates on rescuing that which is lost. Jesus gives a parable here about a man that leaves ninety and nine sheep to go find one that is lost. In a parallel scripture He gives a companion parable about a woman who leaves her purse to hunt for a lost coin. This heavenly meaning behind these earthly stores is that intentional effort must be made to prioritize rescuing those who are lost over those who are secure.

In Matthew 18:15-20 Jesus' focus is on restoring broken relationships. He gives specific five-step instructions about dealing with offenses. First, He says, try to deal with offenses one on one. If that doesn't work try to deal with it with the help of two or three witnesses. If that doesn't work bring it before the church, and if that doesn't work tell it to the church. If the offender is still unrepentant then the church is to excommunicate him while coming into agreement with the church through binding and loosing prayers for the person and wait for the Lord to restore him.

In Matthew 18:21-22 the focus is on radical forgiveness. Peter tries to impress his master by saying, "Lord, how many times shall I forgive my brother when he sins against me? Up to seven times?" Jesus answered, "I tell you, not seven times, but seventy-seven times."

Translators disagree whether Jesus told Peter we need to forgive 70 times or seventy times seven. (490 times) But any attempt to set a certain number of times we need to forgive misses the point of this conversation between Jesus and Peter.

Peter knew that the Talmud determined that a man

may be forgiven his sin the third time but not the fourth. You can almost see Peter's mind spinning. "Well, Jesus always goes beyond the law, so if the law says we need to forgive three times, I will double that and add one for good measure and say 'shall I forgive up to seven times?'" Jesus blew Peter's mucho grande forgiveness out of the water saying "No -- seventy times seven!" The point here is that God calls us to forgive far beyond human reasoning.

I have shared all this to give the proper context for the real focus of this chapter, which is showing the link between torment and unforgiveness. Jesus focused on radical forgiveness with additional insight concerning debt and torment. Even though you may have read these verses several times before, I urge you to read them with fresh eyes. May God quicken your spiritual eyes and understanding to receive new revelation from a familiar text.

> Therefore, the kingdom of heaven is like a king who wanted to settle accounts with his servants. As he began the settlement, a man who owed him ten thousand talents was brought to him. Since he was not able to pay, the master ordered that he and his wife and his children and all that he had be sold to repay the debt. The servant fell on his knees before him. "Be patient with me," he begged, "and I will pay back everything." The servant's master took pity on him, canceled the debt and let him go. But when that servant went out, he found one of his fellow servants who owed him a hundred denarii. He grabbed him and began to choke him. "Pay back what you owe me!" he demanded. His fellow servant fell to his knees and begged him, "Be patient with me, and I will pay you back." But he refused. Instead, he went off and had the man thrown into prison until he could pay the debt. When the other servants saw what had happened, they were

greatly distressed and went and told their master everything that had happened. Then the master called the servant in. "You wicked servant," he said, "I canceled all that debt of yours because you begged me to. Shouldn't you have had mercy on your fellow servant just as I had on you?" *In anger his master turned him over to the jailers to be tortured, until he should pay back all he owed.* This is how my heavenly Father will treat each of you unless you forgive your brother from your heart. Matthew 18:23-35.

Remember that this is given in the context of preservation and restoration. In this text Jesus warns that torment attaches to unforgiveness. He also warns that God's willingness to forgive *us* is linked with *our* willingness to forgive *others*.

Everything in this Matthew 18 is important. Little things from this section can help us understand our need to forgive others.

For example the man who owed 10,000 talents owed the equivalent of millions of dollars and the man who owed him a hundred denarii only owed a few dollars. In essence He is saying that there is no comparison between the little offenses men have committed against one another and the big and little offenses we have committed against the Lord.

God wants us to understand how important it is to release those who have offended us like God has released us from offending him.

There -- a text without a context is a pretext and I didn't want to be guilty of that. Scripture has one correct interpretation but it often has many applications. There is another application of this text that I need to share.

What follows is a key focus of this chapter. Verse 34 of Matthew 18 says something amazing that we will concentrate on, "In anger his master turned him over to the jailers (tormentors, rack) to be tortured, until he should pay back all he owed."

I've read this scripture at least 45 times in my devotions and I always thought this particular one related to a whole different culture and time. In Jesus' day people could be put in debtor's prison and held there until their debt was paid. Roman law allowed a creditor to seize a debtor and place him in jail where he could never repay his loan, and the creditor could take whatever surety there was for the loan to boot. I thought that was then and this is now.

Driving three hours home after doing eight deep healings in two days the Lord said, "I am going to teach you about being held captive to the prison of debt until the last farthing is paid."

It's nice when the Lord shares things like that to make a long drive seem short. I don't take notes when I'm driving so I just listen and ponder what I'm hearing. The Lord showed me that people are still handed over to the tormentors.

Thankfully, in America a lender cannot go to someone's house, arrest the debtor and hold him in prison. But the Lord showed me that many are still held in the prison of debt and tortured by their creditors.

Years ago I was convicted to not go into debt for things of decreasing value. The only hole in my understanding of that was that I thought houses and land would never decrease in value. But Jesus wasn't just talking about monetary debt here. *He was speaking of the debt we owe to God because He forgave us.* That debt obligates us to forgive those who have hurt us.

Jesus made it clear that if we do not forgive others as God has forgiven us that we will be handed over to the tormentors. The actual Greek word that is translated "tormenters" or "jailers" in Matthew 18:34 refers to the rack that was used to torture and torment criminals.

God's schematic for our good is that we forgive all who have hurt us so we will not be given over to torment.

When doing deliverance ministry in the area of forgiveness I have a person grab my wrist and hold it with a tight grip. I explain that I represent the one that offended them and grab their arm and then let go while they are still gripping mine. I tell them to hang on tight and wave my arm back and forth to illustrate that I still have control over them as long as they are holding on to the pain I caused.

Then I explain that the grip of unforgiveness actually creates a soul tie that allows any demons the offender has to flow through the soul tie to torment the one offended.

This is a powerful truth. God's way is for us to forgive all who have offended us so we can be free from torment and demons that take advantage of the soul ties of unforgiveness.

Satan's programming is for us to hang on to offenses so he has permission to torment us and an avenue for his demons to attach.

Chapter 10
From Chaos to Calling

  I began writing this in the fall. As I wrote we were in a season of new beginnings even with winter coming. We had already raked the leaves from the past season and were waiting to clean up those few stubborn leaves that insist on hanging on a little longer. We have some big oak trees that don't lose their leaves until new growth actually pushes the old leaves off. The new beginning actually finalizes death to the previous season as new life overtakes old.

  Genesis is a book of new beginnings. It speaks of the beginning of the earth as we know it, the beginning of light, seasons, animals, birds and fish, stars and mankind. Genesis is the beginning book of God's revelation to man, the beginning of Israel, and the beginning of nations. Genesis is my favorite book to read every year. It contains the beginning of humans, the beginning of sin and the beginning of the Redemption story. Genesis is fascinating to read and I pray that it will be even more fascinating to study. Let's begin with a question. *Beginning of what?* What does God refer to with the first three words of Genesis one?

- In the beginning of what? "<u>In the beginning</u> God created the heaven and the earth. And the earth was without form, and void; and darkness [was] upon the face of the deep. And the Spirit of God moved upon the face of the waters" Genesis 1:1-2. (emphasis mine)

  Genesis 1:1 does not refer to the beginning of God. God, in three persons, has always existed. He is eternal--

without beginning or end. John 1:1 specifically says that Jesus--The Word, The Logos—was already there when the beginning began. In the beginning was the Word, and the Word was with God, and the Word was God. I heard one preacher translate this: "In the beginning was the *thought*."

Genesis 1:1 does not refer to the beginning of Lucifer. Lucifer is really old, but not as old as God. Satan was created by God and was the Chief Musician, created with musical instruments as part of his being. Lucifer was renamed Satan after he fell from heaven. The only place he is called Lucifer is in Isaiah 14:

> "How art thou fallen **from** heaven, O Lucifer, son of the morning! [How] art thou cut down to the ground, which didst weaken the nations! {O Lucifer: or, O day star}   For thou hast said in thine heart, I will ascend **into** heaven, I will exalt my throne above the stars of God: I will sit also upon the mount of the congregation, in the sides of the north: I will ascend above the heights of the clouds; I will be like the most High. Yet thou shalt be brought down to hell, to the sides of the pit." Isaiah 14:12-15.
> (with notes included)

The name Lucifer means "light bearer." After being cast down he was called Satan, which means "accuser or adversary." He is also called devil, dragon, evil one, god of this world, Beelzebub and a host of other unsavory names. Jesus simply called him "Satan" when he described his fall from heaven:

> "And he said unto them, I beheld Satan as lightning fall from heaven." Luke 10:18.

So when was Satan kicked out of heaven? I spent hours studying what different scholars think about this. Many say he was kicked out of heaven at the beginning of the Church Age. They try to use Revelation 12 to prove their point. But that can't be, because Satan was Job's adversary and Job is considered the oldest book of the Bible--written even before the Genesis account was put in writing. Besides that, Satan tempted Adam and Eve on earth in Genesis 3.

I personally believe that Satan was kicked out of heaven before the earth as we know it was recreated. He tempted man in the garden--before man sinned so "In the beginning" cannot refer to Satan.

Genesis 1:1 does not refer to the beginning of demons. Without giving the full context of Revelation 12:3-9, let me tell you that one third of the angels of heaven were taken out by the dragon. Verse three said that the dragon swept one third of the "stars" out of heaven. The stars refer to angelic messengers.

> "And the great dragon was cast out, that old serpent, called the Devil, and Satan, which deceiveth the whole world: he was cast out into the earth, and his angels were cast out with him." Revelation 12:9 KJV.

But when did this happen? Genesis 1:1 does not refer to the beginning of chaos. A deeper look at verse 2 shows that the earth was without form, and void; and darkness [was] upon the face of the deep. Let's take a look at those words.

Without form: This word comes from an unused root meaning to lay waste; and is translated: vain, vanity, confusion, without form, wilderness, naught, nothing, empty place, and waste. It is defined as:
1) formlessness, confusion, unreality, emptiness, stupor of this generation.
   1a) formlessness (of primeval earth)
   1a1) nothingness, empty space

1b) that which is empty or unreal (of idols)
1c) wasteland, wilderness (of solitary places)
1d) place of chaos (world as it was "in the beginning")
1e) vanity.

<u>Void:</u> This word comes from an unused root meaning "to be empty" and is translated: void or emptiness. It is defined as: emptiness, void, waste.

<u>Deep:</u> This word is translated deep, depth, and deep places.
It is defined:
1) deep, depths, deep places, abyss, the deep, sea
1a) deep (of subterranean waters)
1b) deep, sea, abysses (of sea)
1c) primeval ocean, deep
1d) deep, depth (of river)
1e) abyss, Sheol

We can't be sure when the substance of the earth was formed--but we know that "the earth was without form, and void; and darkness [was] upon the face of the deep." as the Spirit of God was hovering over it. Something was there, but it lacked clear form, purpose, focus and light.

Now transition your thinking from the earth to it human inhabitants. Before Christ comes into a life a person lacks clear form, purpose, focus and light. That remains true for Believers in any area not submitted to the Lord Jesus. The Holy Spirit hovers over us but we are in a darkened form until the light of Christ comes in to a person or situation.

Consider the note added by the translator of the NIV:

⸱ "Now the earth was {Or possibly became} formless and empty, darkness was over the surface of the deep, and the Spirit of God was hovering over the waters."
Genesis 1:2. (with note in brackets)

The translators saw something that we should consider. Satan was kicked out of heaven before man was created. The earth, as we know it, had not yet been created--but something was there. Note that Genesis 1:2 says that the earth *"WAS."* We don't know what it was before man was created or before Satan was cast down to it, but whatever that something was, it had become formless and empty and darkness was over the surface of the deep.

Are you with me so far? I suspect that whatever the earth was became messed up when Satan came into it and part of God's redemptive plan for the earth was to create humans in his own likeness to execute His dominion rather than Satan's dominion over the earth.

Genesis 1:1 does not refer to the beginning spiritual warfare. Genesis begins with the contrast between chaos and order, darkness and light, formlessness and form, emptiness and fullness. It looked like Satan was winning because he had killed, stolen, and destroyed whatever God's plan was for the earth: "so again the earth was {Or possibly became} formless and empty, darkness was over the surface of the deep, and the Spirit of God was hovering over the waters."

Verse 2 ends with the declaration that the Spirit of God was hovering over whatever was already there, waiting for God to speak order and goodness into it. That makes me think that "in the beginning" refers to the beginning of God's plan to redeem the earth through the dominion of people created in his own image.

Chapter 11
The Battle over Abundance

Early in the last chapter I asked, "Beginning of what?" and concluded with my thought that it was the beginning of God's redemptive plan for earth. Now let me divert your attention to a similar question. When did Jesus' plan for abundant life begin for mankind and when did Satan's plan to kill, steal, and destroy begin? Did the truth, plan and impact of John 10:10 begin when Jesus created the world or only after he came into that which was His own and His own received him not?

> The thief comes only to steal and kill and destroy; I have come that they may have life, and have it to the full. John 10:10.

It appears that God's blueprint for abundance and Satan's programming for desolation were already planned even before the creation of man. The two opposing forces are seen from the beginning: God's blueprint and destiny for you or the Devil's programming and determination against you.

There are a host of Scriptures that refer to God's work and good plan for each individual:

> My frame was not hidden from you when I was made in the secret place. When I was woven together in the depths of the earth, your eyes saw my unformed body. All the days ordained for me were written in your book before one of them came to be. How precious to {Or concerning} me are your thoughts, O God! How vast is the sum of them! Psalm 139:15-17. (NIV note in brackets)

⸱ Before I formed you in the womb I knew {or chose} you, before you were born I set you apart; I appointed you as a prophet to the nations. Jeremiah 1:5 (NIV note in brackets)

⸱ "For I know the plans I have for you," declares the LORD, "plans to prosper you and not to harm you, plans to give you hope and a future." Jeremiah 29:11.

⸱ For we are God's workmanship, created in Christ Jesus to do good works, which God prepared in advance for us to do. Ephesians 2:10.

The devil's purpose is to destroy God's destiny for people through his diabolical schematics. When he comes to kill, steal and destroy he really doesn't care that much about people. What he really hates is God's image in people and the authority and dominion God gives those who truly follow Jesus Christ. Second Corinthians 4:4 speaks of the veil that he puts on people to keep them from seeing God's Good news. Second Corinthians 10:4-5 speaks of the schematics, logic systems and strongholds that Satan tries to use to keep us from entering in.

While I was first working on this, I ministered deep healing to a woman from Stockholm, Sweden. I was doing my first phone appointment with her and was determined to get to the bottom of things. We spent 80 minutes on the phone working deep healing, and only made it through the point of conception.

The Holy Spirit revealed so many areas where Satan had taken legal right through the sins of her ancestors to kill, steal, and destroy. I had actually scheduled 2 hours with her but cut it 40 minutes short, because so much power had gone out from me. She needed to realize that her Heavenly Father is bigger than her earthly father. So do we.

> Jesus came to destroy the devil's works:
> But you know that he appeared so that he might take away our sins. And in him is no sin. No one who lives in him keeps on sinning. No one who continues to sin has either seen him or known him. Dear children, do not let anyone lead you astray. He who does what is right is righteous, just as he is righteous. He who does what is sinful is of the devil, because the devil has been sinning from the beginning. **The reason the Son of God appeared was to destroy the devil's work**. No one who is born of God will continue to sin, because God's seed remains in him; he cannot go on sinning, because he has been born of God. This is how we know who the children of God are and who the children of the devil are: Anyone who does not do what is right is not a child of God; nor is anyone who does not love his brother. 1 John 3:5-10.

Jesus came to destroy the devil's works in people through His shed blood on the cross. The good news of the Gospel is that Jesus lived a perfect life and was without sin. On the cross he took our sin upon his own body. He died a horrendous death and paid our eternal penalty of sin by going to hell, where he preached to the departed spirits of those in prison. Then he rose from the dead and triumphed over the powers of darkness, making a public spectacle of them. Hallelujah--now everyone who follows Jesus as Lord has or can have victory over sin and the devil!

Jesus came to destroy the devil's work in the world and continues doing so through his Church. The Book of Genesis is the beginning of God's story of how far He is willing to go to redeem humans and how badly He wants humans to multiply and take dominion of the earth for His glory. We can read about that in Genesis and Revelation and in most of the books in between. We will dig deeper in the following chapters as we look at the first count of creation.

For now it is important to understand Jesus came to move people from chaos to calling. He came and was anointed to transform us (life, marriage, family) from fragmentation to wholeness. He has already taken the first step in creation and on the cross. But He leaves the next step up to us. Jesus paid the way through His cross and we pave the way through our own crosses.

> Then said Jesus to his disciples, "If any one doth will to come after me, let him disown himself, and take up his cross, and follow me, for whoever may will to save his life, shall lose it, and whoever may lose his life for my sake shall find it, for what is a man profited if he may gain the whole world, but of his life suffer loss? or what shall a man give as an exchange for his life? For, the Son of Man is about to come in the glory of his Father, with his messengers, and then he will reward each, according to his work." Matthew 16:24-27 YLT.

Jesus did not go to the cross so we wouldn't have to. He did some things there that we cannot do for ourselves. But He went there to make it possible for *us* to get to the cross. We are called to assassinate the rebel within by carrying the cross He assigns for each disciple to carry.

Chapter 12
Treasures for Personal Transformation

I took notes from Chuck Pierce in the front of my "preaching" Bible in Genesis 1. In Genesis 1:2, I noted that God comes to places where darkness is over the surface of the deep. In my old religious thinking I believed that God only came to places of light and purity, but as I studied the Scriptures I've finally realized that God intentionally goes to places of darkness to release His light. He even sent Abram from the land of goodness and safety into the land where the most detestable practices were observed in religion and relationships.

Next I noted from Chuck that God began to speak and recreate the form of that which was messed up. The Spirit of God hovered over the darkness of that which was messed up until God released the prophetic word that straightened things up. Having done that, God created people with dominating authority to be fruitful, multiply, fill the earth and subdue it through godly rule.

A Treasure Hunt

Let's go on a treasure hunt and see how the first account of creation speaks to what God is NOW creating in us as we transition into Kingdom Life.

First note the word translated "God" in these verses. It is the plural "Elohim" which is usually translated "God" in the Old Testament. God the Father, God the Son and God the Holy Spirit were active in all of creation. Who was God speaking to when He spoke in the creation story?

He was speaking both to the other persons of the Trinity and to that which was being created.

> And God said, "Let there be light," and there was light. God saw that the light was good, and he separated the light from the darkness. God called the light "day," and the darkness he called night." And there was evening, and there was morning--the first day." Genesis 1:3-5.

God thought of light but it was not created until he spoke it. He called light good but he did not call darkness good. In his very first act of Creation of the earth he separated light from darkness. Notice that God's day goes from evening to morning. In every case he begins speaking new things into existence in the evening.

Could it be that part of the chaos we experience is because we think our day begins in the morning rather than allowing God to speak things into order in the evening? Years ago I began creating my "to do" list in the evening and my work list before I left the office each day. It worked really well, though I confess that I often let busyness keep me from doing this before I left the office or went to bed, so I frequently began the next day with no sense of order. Doing that bred chaos, which is the opposite of the divine order God wants to speak into our lives. So let's look for treasures.

Treasures to Practice:

<u>Treasure One:</u> If we follow God's example we will begin speaking in the evening what we want to accomplish in the morning.

> And God said, "Let there be an expanse between the waters to separate water from water." So God made the expanse and separated the water under the expanse from the water above it. And it was so. God called the expanse "sky." And there was evening, and there was morning-- the second day. Genesis 1:6-8.

Have you ever considered how God created everything in proper order? Long before humans understood the working of light and tides or the way the atmosphere gathers water through evaporation only to release them upon thirsty land, God created the atmosphere of the earth and inspired someone (probably Moses) to write about it centuries before meteorologists gained understanding about it.

<u>Treasure Two:</u> The understanding of what God does often comes later. Walking in faith is doing what God says even before you understand it.

> And God said, "Let the water under the sky be gathered to one place, and let dry ground appear." And it was so. God called the dry ground "land," and the gathered waters he called "seas." And God saw that it was good. Then God said, "Let the *land produce* vegetation: seed-bearing plants and trees on the land that bear fruit with seed in it, according to their various kinds." And it was so. The *land produced* vegetation: plants bearing seed according to their kinds and trees bearing fruit with seed in it according to their kinds. And God saw that it was good. And there was evening, and there was morning--the third day.
> Genesis 1:9-13.

We now know how important water is to all living things. On the third day God first created seas and land.

Notice <u>who</u> produced the vegetation. In verse 11 God said, "Let the land produce" and in verse 12 it says "the land produced vegetation."

How can land create anything? How does dirt turn a radish seed into a radish? Can you do that? You can plant a kernel of corn, but can you transform a single corn seed into a plant with 1-2 ears full of delicious kernels?

Which came first: the seed or the plant? Actually the land came first and God gave the dirt the inherent ability to produce vegetation and fruit. That is too wonderful to understand!

<u>Treasure Three:</u> When God speaks a thing He releases the inner ability to accomplish the thing. "God's calling IS God's enabling."

> And God said, "Let there be lights in the expanse of the sky to separate the day from the night, and let them serve as signs to mark seasons and days and years, and let them be lights in the expanse of the sky to give light on the earth." And it was so. God made two great lights--the greater light to govern the day and the lesser light to govern the night. He also made the stars. God set them in the expanse of the sky to give light on the earth, to **govern** the day and the night, and to separate light from darkness. And God saw that it was good. And there was evening, and there was morning--the fourth day. Genesis 1:14-19.
> (emphasis mine)

These verses record how God made calendars possible. He set seasons in order according to the Sun and moon and the Hebrew calendar still goes by the time and seasons that God ordained. That is why many Believers try to observe significant Jewish holy days to come into sync with God's timing.

Do you see how God set the sun and the moon to **govern or rule** the day and the night? From the beginning God intended to rule -- even the day and night in a way that was good.

It's interesting that the legislature decided the way God rules or governs the time isn't good enough for them? Therefore government created "Daylight Savings Time" (some people call it silly season) so people could live out their busy lives unhindered with the order that God intended the sun and moon to exercise.

I am being precocious concerning Eastern Standard Daylight Savings time, but could it be that we have been so lawless that we won't even accept time the way God created it? Does resisting His created order bring further chaos in our lives and homes?

Treasure Four: God's order comes and chaos breaks off when we move into God's kairos (opportune) timing.

> And God said, "Let the water teem with living creatures, and let birds fly above the earth across the expanse of the sky." So God created the great creatures of the sea and every living and moving thing with which the water teems, according to their kinds, and every winged bird according to its kind. And God saw that it was good. God **blessed** them and said, "Be fruitful and increase in number and fill the water in the seas, and let the birds increase on the earth." And there was evening, and there was morning--the fifth day. Genesis 1:20-23.

Do you see what is added here? God did not bless the day or the night. He did not bless the water of the heavens or earth. There is no mention of him blessing the ground or vegetation when he created it. He did not bless the moon or the sun. But here in verse 22 we see that God blessed the living creatures.

Have you ever noticed that before? The first blessing of God was reserved for living birds and sea creatures. The earliest blessing was not for the planets or even the plants. Blessing began with the first hearts.

<u>Treasure Five:</u> God's intends to bless living creatures.

Therefore he wants *us* to bless living creatures. Think about it. Jesus said that even a sparrow does not fall to the ground without the Father's notice. I remember a verse from Proverbs in the Living Bible that implied if a man is righteous even his animal's benefit.

<u>Treasure Six:</u> If you have a heart God wants to bless it.

Satan wants to curse, lead us into temptation and condemn us when we fail. A young man who failed in his marriage covenant asked if he had lost his chance of going to heaven. He was beating himself up so much that the devil hardly had to help.

But Satan's schematic is to knock us down and keep us down while God's is to pick us up and keep us up. I referred the young man to a glorious Scripture where Paul lists all sorts of deviant behaviors and then says "and that is what *some of you were.* But you were washed, you were sanctified, you were justified in the name of the Lord Jesus Christ and by the Spirit of our God." (1 Corinthians 6:11)

Back to Genesis: God said "let the **LAND** produce living creatures . . . ." People used to understand this dust to dust concept better than we do today. Funeral committals used to include the phrase "from dust to dust." That reminds me of one girl that went home from church contemplating how the preacher said from dust we come and to dust we go.

That night she woke up screaming, "Mommy -- Mommy -- somebody's either coming or going under my bed!"

Beginning in the 1970's the United States, and now much of the world celebrates Earth Day. At times it sounds idolatrous like people are worshipping "Mother Earth" rather than serving the One who created the earth. The Mother Earth people may emphasize the value of the creation over the Creator. But Believers may be guilty of overlooking how valuable the land is in God's eyes.

> And God said, "Let the *land* produce living creatures according to their kinds: livestock, creatures that move along the ground, and wild animals, each according to its kind." And it was so. God made the wild animals according to their kinds, the livestock according to their kinds, and all the creatures that move along the ground according to their kinds. *And God saw that it was good.* Genesis 1:24-25. (emphasis mine)

During the latter part of the 20th Century scientists began to research the power of DNA. Every year brings breakthrough in medicine and criminology because of new things that are being learned about DNA.

But, nearly 6,000 years ago (in my humble opinion) God created the DNA of every type of creature so they could all produce after their own kind.

People ask: "what came first, the chicken or the egg?" Genesis is clear: God created the chicken first with the ability to produce eggs to reproduce more chickens--all with the same DNA.

You may think that carbon-dating has proven that certain fossils are billions of years old. I don't buy that and I believe the Jewish calendar gives a more accurate accounting of time than evolutionists do.

But consider the following. When God created the cow, did he create a cow or a calf? And when he created the horse did he create a horse or a colt? And when he created the frog and the fish, did he create an egg or creatures that hop or swim? And when he created man did he create a baby or an adult?

Genesis indicates that God created everything in its mature form. Not a monkey that turned into a man but a monkey that reproduced monkeys and people that reproduced people, each after its own God-designed DNA. Now let's go a step further. When God created the earth did he create a baby earth or a mature earth?

If God created a cow rather than a calf, and a horse rather than a colt and a frog and a fish rather than an egg and an adult rather than a child and a mature earth rather than an infant earth, is it not possible that he created an earth that was billions of years old on the day it was created?

Treasure Seven: Within all creation God placed the principle of multiplication according to specific DNA:
- Then God said, "Let us make man in **our** image, in **our** likeness." Genesis 1:26a. (emphasis mine)

More on DNA later. For now I ask you to note the use of the first person plural here. God in three persons said "Let US make man in OUR image and in OUR likeness. God's plan is and always has been that people share His image and His likeness in the World.

Satan's chief interest in people is to kill, steal, and destroy God's image, glory and likeness from them. That is why he tempts people to sin because God doesn't sin, so when people sin it destroys His likeness in them.

In the beginning God created man to reflect His own image and glory but since Adam's fall have sinned and fallen far short of God's glory.
> For all have sinned and fall short of the
> glory of God. Romans 3:23.

It is clear that people have fallen short of the glory of God. But Jesus became sin that we might become the righteousness of God. He lived, died and rose again that we might regain the glory and image of God.
> We know that we live in him and he in us, because he has
> given us of his Spirit. In this way, love is made complete
> among us so that we will have confidence on the day of
> judgment, because in this world we are like him.
> 1 John 4:13, 17.

<u>Treasure Eight</u>: God desires for His image and His likeness to reflect through Humans! As supreme ruler God designed humans to rule and to reign.
> And let them rule over the fish of the sea and the birds of
> the air, over the livestock, over all the earth, and over all
> the creatures that move along the ground. Genesis 1:26b.

One horrible effect of sin is that people caught in sin are driven, rather than called. They exercise what they consider personal freedom which leads to bondage. God created us to rule--not to be ruled. Kingdom people, in submission to the Lord, are to drive the world, not vice versa. God created us to be fruitful like trees planted by streams of water, not directionless, like chaff driven by the wind. I absolutely love what Jack Hayford wrote below:

<u>Treasure Nine:</u> Genesis is wrapped in the truth that God created humankind as partners, not as peons.

(Jack Hayford, <u>Hayford's Bible Handbook</u>, Thomas Nelson Publisher 1995 bottom of pages 2-3)

Pay attention! God wants to do new things in our lives, families and churches. But we have entered a season, preceding the last Great Awakening, where God only creates what will reflect His Image and His Glory. We are in a season where we are called to move from Romans 3:23 where we have *fallen* from His glory, to 1 John 4:17 where we *reflect* His glory!

> For all have sinned and fall short of the glory of God. Romans 3:23.

> We know that we live in Him, and He in us, because he has given us of his Spirit. In this way, love is made complete among us so that we will have confidence on the Day of Judgment, because in this world we are like him. 1 John 4:13, 17.

Chapter 13
Moving from Sin to Glory

Thousands flocked to Billy Graham's altars singing his favorite altar call hymn "Just as I am without one plea." That's a great place to start but a horrible place to stay. Evangelists lament that so many pray "the prayer" but do not grow on to faithfulness and fruitfulness.

Thank the Lord that He meets us "just as I am" but he doesn't want to leave us as we were. He wants to transform us into His own glorious image.

Genesis three is clear that humans were created in the image of God.

> So God created man in his own image, in the image of God he created him; male and female he created them.
> Genesis 1:27.

Even though the last part of verse 27 makes it clear that both men and women are created in the image of God it is important to understand the fourth word of verse 27 — "man." The word translated "man" in English, is "Adam" in Hebrew. Adam is a generic term for humans and is not gender specific. The word "human" comes from a root that is translated: multitude 70 times, abundance 35, great 9, greatness 8, much 8, abundantly 4, plenty 3, many 3, long 2, excellent 1, and miscellaneous 12 times.

The word translated "abundance" is defined: 1) multitude, abundance, greatness; 1a) multitude; 1a1) abundance, abundantly and 1a2) numerous. Therefore, when God created humans, both male and female, He created them to have and enjoy life more abundantly. That is God's schematic for people!

Satan's chief schematic for people is to kill, steal, and to destroy God's image, glory, and likeness from them. Therefore he tempts people to sin because God doesn't sin and sin destroys His likeness in them.

When we sin we fall short of the glory of God. In other words, sin makes us fall short of the image of God. When we fall short of God's glory we also fall short of His blueprint for our lives. We fall away from the abundance God wants us to have and into the loss that Satan uses to strip people of God's image and blessing. As Jesus said:

> The thief comes only to steal and kill and destroy; I have come that they may have life, and have it to the full. "I am the good shepherd. The good shepherd lays down his life for the sheep. John 10:10-11.

Here is an important principle of restoring abundance that applies to every person, marriage, family, church, community, state, and nation. To restore the abundance of God is to restore His image and that is what advancing the Kingdom of God is about!

It is time to focus on one major topic: understanding and restoring God's image in our lives and world.

We Were Created in the Image of God

Humans were created in the image of God. But what does that mean? First, since God is creator, in His image we are created creators. God created the world and everything that is in it. Then he made man in His own image. Only humans have the creative image of God.

There is no end to the creativity of man. In my lifetime men have created amazing things: color television, computers, laptops, cell phone, gaming systems, iPod's and iPhone's, technology for man to walk on the moon, DNA testing, McDonald's drive-through restaurants, disposable diapers and razors, GPS, smart bombs--- the list could go on and on--but that might make me feel old.

But there's a problem. Man's creative nature has fallen short of God's creative image. When God looked at what He created in Genesis One He said, "It is good." But can we say "it is good" to things that people have created apart from God's image? Is the "morning after" birth control pill good? Are weapons of mass destruction good?

To restore man's abundance we must restore God's creative image. When people carry that creative image they will advance the Kingdom of God in every part of society.

Restoring Man's Abundance through Dominion.

God is sovereign; in His image we are sovereign. When God created humans, He gave them dominion over the animals, the birds of the air, and the fish of the sea. He told man to tend the earth and take care of it. God wanted people to be stewards of the earth for God.

The reason God created humans in His sovereign image was so they would extend His rule throughout the earth. But as people have lost God's sovereign image, the earth subsequently lost God's abundance.

An important key to restoring earth's abundance is to restore people to God's sovereign image. When that happens, people will advance the Kingdom of God!

Restoring Man's Triune Nature.

God is triune and in His image humans are triune.

The Godhead consists of three persons: God the Father, God the Son and God the Holy Spirit. Though the word

"Trinity" is not found in the Bible, the Godhead--three in one--is mentioned repeatedly. Jesus said things like "I am in my Father and He is in me," and "Anyone who has seen me has seen the Father."

All three persons of the Trinity were present in creation and in Jesus' baptism. When Jesus came up from the water "to fulfill all righteousness" the Father spoke of his pleasure from heaven and the Spirit landed on Him in the form of a dove. The doctrine of the Trinity is a litmus test of true biblical Christianity.

In God's image people have three parts: spirit, soul and body. One key of restoring man's abundance is to restore the triune image of God.

While looking at Ray Stedman's thoughts from www.raystedman.org/leadership/smith/dyingtolive/ch10.html I found the following diagram on the web from Bob Smith's book <u>Dying to Live</u>. Bob is a Peninsula Bible Church Founding Father and writes on Biblical Counseling Principles. First published 1976.

DIAGRAM A

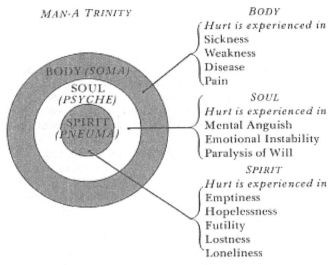

The *SOURCE* of the problem may be in any of these three realms, but the *HURT* affects the *WHOLE PERSON*.

God the Father, God the Son and God the Holy Spirit are triune and keep in perfect balance. Each person of the Godhead is distinct yet one. Their perfect balance and oneness reflect the glory of the image of God in three persons.

People are created in God's triune image but are prone to imbalance. They may be so spiritual that they are no worldly good. Or they may be so soulish that they do not understand spiritual truths. Or they may simply be driven by their physical desires with little concern for their soul or spirit.

As an intern with Youth for Christ in the early 70's I learned how they used Luke 2:52 as a pivotal verse to explain the need for balance between the mental, physical, spiritual and social aspects of life.

 ⸭ And Jesus grew in wisdom and stature,
    and in favor with God and men. Luke 2:52.

They rightly taught that Jesus should be Lord of all four of these aspects. So that places great emphasis on His Spirit in our spirits as the leading force of all that we are.

Regenerated and born again spirits:
1. Communicate with God:

⸙ The Spirit himself testifies with our spirit that we are God's children. Romans 8:16.

People cannot even be born again unless the Holy Spirit draws them to Jesus. He speaks to them of their need and after they are born again He speaks to them of His lead. Unfortunately, religious people and religious spirits try to keep Believers from hearing God's voice.

2. Are saved for the day of the Lord:

⸙ Hand this man over to Satan, so that the sinful nature may be destroyed and his spirit saved on the day of the Lord. 1 Corinthians 5:5.

When people are truly born again the Holy Spirit is in them for the long haul. About the only way to make Him leave is to purposely reject him. Paul instructed the Corinthian Church to put a man out of the church whose behavior was more perverse than worldly people. But Paul still had confidence that the Lord would use that discipline to bring him to repentance. (See 1 Corinthians five and 2 Corinthians 2:5-11)

3. Make us <u>ONE</u> With Christ:

⸙ But he who unites himself with the Lord is one with him in the Spirit. 1 Corinthians 6:17.

are two Greek words translated "another" but different meanings. One means "another of a [kin]d." For example: "Apples are one kind of fruit and orange other." But the other word really means "another of the *same* kind." For example: "Here is one red delicious apple and here is another red delicious apple." When Jesus said the Father would send another comforter he used the word that means another of the same kind. So we are one with Jesus in and through His "another of the same kind Spirit."

4. Have God's DNA:
- For you have been born again, not of perishable seed) but of imperishable, through the living and enduring word of God. 1 Peter 1:23.

- No one who is born of God will continue to sin, because God's seed remains in him; he cannot go on sinning, because he has been born of God. 1 John 3:9.

These verses are exciting because the Greek word translated "seed" in these verses is "sperma" or "sperm." We know that sperm carries DNA, so when people are born again they take on their heavenly Father's DNA.

5. Are radically saved, changed, empowered and anointed:
- Therefore, if anyone is in Christ, he is a new creation; the old has gone, the new has come! 2 Corinthians 5:17.

Do you feel the old has gone and the new has come in your life? Man's regenerated spirit is made perfect—justified--it never sins and cannot sin because God lives in the regenerated spirit. God's image is stamped on the regenerated spirit -- His love is shed abroad in the spirit. But we have a problem: we do not always walk according to the spirit. Sometimes we walk according to the soul. Even the Apostle Paul lamented about the battle between his spirit and flesh in Romans chapter seven.

Satan cannot destroy the work of God in the spirit of a human, unless he or she becomes apostate. God's abundance is released within the spirit when a person is born again. Unfortunately we have trouble working the new image of God within our spirits to our souls and bodies. Therefore the thief wants to kill, steal, and destroy God's image in our souls. Our soul is our mind, will, emotions and memories. Our soul determines the way we think, choose and feel.

- Do not be afraid of those who can kill the body but cannot kill the soul. Rather, be afraid of the One who can destroy both soul (psyche) and body in hell. Matthew 10:28. (note is mine)

- What good will it be for a man if he gains the whole world, yet forfeits his soul? Or what can a man give in exchange for his soul (psyche)? Matthew 16:26. (note is mine)

- He answered: "Love the Lord your God with all your heart and with all your soul (psyche) and with all your strength and with all your mind; and, Love your neighbor as *yourself.* Luke 10:27. (note and emphasis mine)

- For the word of God is living and active. Sharper than any double-edged sword, it penetrates even to dividing soul and spirit, joints and marrow; it judges the thoughts and attitudes of the heart. Hebrews 4:12.

God's abundance is released by bringing spirit, soul and body all the way into God's image. Satan's havoc is released when we fall out of God's image and likeness.

People can lose God's image and likeness:
1. They can lose His likeness in their bodies.
⸱ Therefore God gave them over in the sinful desires of their hearts to sexual impurity for the degrading of their bodies with one another. Romans 1:24

All sexual sin is an attack against God's image in the body. God's image is pure and promiscuity is unholy.

2. They can lose His likeness in their souls.
⸱ Because of this, God gave them over to shameful lusts. Romans 1:27.

All sexual perversion including pornography, sodomy, perversity, pedophilia and the like is an attack against God's image in the soul.
⸱ Furthermore, since they did not think it worthwhile to retain the knowledge of God, he gave them over to a depraved mind, to do what ought not to be done. Romans 1:28.

The Greek word "Nous" is here translated "mind" or "reprobate mind" but this goes deeper than just our gray matter. It means "mind or disposition" in the sense of inner orientation or moral attitude. It controls the subconscious mind that controls about 80% of our actions and reactions.

All religious adultery is an attack against God's image in the spirit. Please note that God gives people up in this order; first in body, then in soul, and finally in spirit.

Three Major Categories of People

There are three major categories of people in Scripture: spiritual, soulish and reprobate. The first one we will look at is the spiritual person.

1. Spiritual People:

> The spiritual (pneumatikos) man makes judgments about all things, but he himself is not subject to any man's judgment: "For who has known the mind of the Lord that he may instruct him?" But we have the mind of Christ. Brothers, I could not address you as spiritual (pneumatikos) but as worldly (sarkinos)--mere infants in Christ. 1 Corinthians 2:15-3:1. (notes mine)

I inserted the Greek word "pneumatikos" that is translated "spiritual" here and other places and will include it in its different forms in the Scriptures used in this section.

> Brothers, if someone is caught in a sin, you who are spiritual (pneumatikoi) should restore him gently. But watch yourself, or you also may be tempted. Galatians 6:1. (notes mine)

A spiritual person's human spirit is strongest. It exercises leadership and control over their soul and body. Therefore their soul is kept in check by their human spirit and their body is held in subjection to their soul.

2. Soulish people—a lukewarm, carnal, or sin controlled Believer:

> The man without the Spirit (psuchikos) does not accept the things that come from the Spirit of God, for they are foolishness to him, and he cannot understand them, because they are spiritually discerned. 1 Corinthians 2:14. (note mine)

I inserted the Greek word "psuchikos" which is translated "the man without the Spirit" here. I believe "soulish" is a better translation.

A soulish person's spirit is weaker and their soul (the sensual mind, will, emotions and memories) grows stronger. Their physical (sensual) fights for control. At this point the two opposing forces of spirituality and sensuality result in double-mindedness and instability. James says we become double-souled.

> He is a double-minded (dipsukos) man, unstable in all he does. James 1:8. (note mine)

I inserted the Greek word "dipsukos" which is translated "double-minded" because it literally means having "two (or divided) souls." This speaks of having a "fragmented soul" that is heading in different directions at the same time. The common condition of having fragmented souls is part of Satan's schematic to bring chaos rather than order to a person's life. Most people have some fragmentation of soul and people with D.I.D. are greatly fragmented. Thank God that Jesus came to heal the fragmented heart!

3. Reprobate people:

> They profess that they know God; but in works they deny [him], being abominable, and disobedient, and unto every good work reprobate. Titus 1:16 KJV.

Reprobate means "void of judgment." A reprobate's spirit is quenched; the soul becomes philosophical or religious with no connection with the mind of Christ that Paul says spiritual people have. The reprobate's body becomes sensual and often perverted as well.

We filter all incoming data either through our spirit, soul or body and that controls how easily we receive revelation. If we receive through our spirits, we can easily receive the things of the spirit. If we receive through our soul or body it becomes easier to receive sensual data.

We have been in a great war concerning worship for some time now and we have attributed that war to Satan and his demons and they probably play a part in it. But as I observe the opponents in the worship battle they seem to fall into three categories. Spiritual people understand where the Spirit of God is leading, so they are willing to walk into uncharted territory just to keep in step with the Spirit. Soulish people, on the other hand, want things to make sense to their mind, will and emotions. Therefore they end up resisting God Himself so their souls remain in control. And sensual people simply want what makes them feel good. This struggle to make things fit according to the spiritual, soulish or sensual nature is why there are so many worship wars in churches

GOD'S CURE FOR REBROBATION:
1. The Spirit Can Be Born Again!

> Flesh gives birth to flesh, but the Spirit gives birth to spirit. You should not be surprised at my saying, "You must be born again." John 3:6-7.

It has to start here! God restores people from the inside out. At the center of each person is the very life of the person--the spirit. Until a person is born again his or her spirit is lost and under the control of the ruler of this world. (Eph. 2:1-3)

But when they are born again, God's Spirit brings life to them by taking up residence in their human spirits. (Romans 8:9) This is instantaneous and happens when they are born again.

2. The Soul Can Be Saved.

After our spirits are born again, the Holy Spirit in our spirits begins working on our souls. Remember, the soul is our mind, will and emotions. After we are born again in spirit our souls are *being* converted. This "saving of our souls" is a process that begins when we are born again, accelerates when we are sanctified and filled with the Spirit, and continues until we are glorified.

- For you are receiving the goal of your faith,
  the salvation of your souls. 1 Peter 1:9.
- Wherefore lay apart all filthiness and superfluity of naughtiness, and receive with meekness the engrafted word, <u>which is able to save your souls</u>. James 1:21 KJV.

3. The Body Can Be Crucified and Will Be Redeemed.

While we remain on earth we are to "reckon ourselves dead to sin" by "crucifying our bodies with Christ." This is an act of faith whereby we identify with the death of Jesus on the cross. The glorification of our bodies will take place at the rapture of the church.

- Do you not know that your body is a temple of the Holy Spirit, who is in you, who you have received of God?
  You are not your own; you were bought at a price.
  Therefore honor God with your body.
  1 Corinthians 6:19-20.

Let's quickly review. We were created in God's image. God is triune as Father, Son and Holy Spirit. We are triune with spirit, soul and body. Sin causes us to lose God's image in our spirit, soul and body. People lose God's image to the degree they have ignored God and His holy will for their lives. God still desires to restore us to His image. He calls us to be born again in spirit, converted in soul and crucified with Christ. God wants us to be like Jesus!

⸸ We know that we live in him and he in us, because he has given us of his Spirit. In this way, love is made complete among us so that we will have confidence on the Day of Judgment, because in this world we are like him.
1 John 4:13, 17.

Jesus' schematic is to restore God's image in people.
⸸ Be perfect, therefore, as your heavenly Father is perfect.
Matthew 5:48.

⸸ Because by one sacrifice he has made perfect forever those who are being made holy. Hebrews 10:24.

    A great spiritual battle that rages within Believers is: God's Spirit in our spirit prompting us to holiness versus Sin and Satan prompting us to ungodliness. The winning side is determined by whichever side we join!
    Satan's schematic is to lure us to destruction through disobedience.
⸸ Rebellion is (as) the sin of witchcraft
1 Samuel 15:23a KJV.

⸸ Be self-controlled and alert. Your enemy the devil prowls around like a roaring lion looking for someone to devour. 1 Peter 5:8.

    We find protection through obeying God.
    God will never bless disobedience. He always blesses obedience. God wants to develop the character in every person. He will give a person a test and if they pass it, He blesses them. But if they don't pass it, He gives them another test. God does this for our good so we might be conformed to the image of Christ.

> See, I am setting before you today a blessing and a curse--the blessing if you obey the commands of the LORD your God that I am giving you today, the curse if you disobey the commands of the LORD your God and turn from the way that I command you today by following other gods, which you have not known. Deuteronomy 11:26-28.

We find protection through God's Word. In Revelation 12:11, Jesus says that we overcome Satan by the blood of the Lamb and the word of our testimony.
> And take the helmet of salvation, and the sword (rhema) of the Spirit, which is the word of God. Ephesians 6:17. (note mine)

We also find protection by properly submitting to those in authority. We never lose our personal sovereignty. The choice is ours. We can rebel and leave God's umbrella of protection or repent and come under proper authority. We have great protection when we walk in proper submission but are a target for the enemy when we rebel.

God's plan is for our good. God's schematic is to give us a hope and a future! That is a needed message for our defeated and hopeless generation.
> For I know the plans I have for you, declares the LORD, "Plans to prosper you and not to harm you, plans to give you hope and a future. Jeremiah 29:11.

God's plan is to sanctify us through and through!

> May God himself, the God of peace, sanctify you through and through. May your whole spirit, soul and body be kept blameless at the coming of our Lord Jesus Christ. 1 Thessalonians 5:23.

To sanctify means to make holy. It carries the idea of an ordinary man or woman coming out of a life of sin and being transformed from glory unto glory and prepared to do works of ministry. It is a process whereby we can break down every stronghold of the enemy and walk in freedom with Christ. Sanctification is clearly God's will for every Christian.

> It is God's will that you should be sanctified: that you should avoid sexual immorality; that each of you should learn to control his own body in a way that is holy and honorable. 1 Thessalonians 4:3.

Chapter 14
Three Types of People

Every person fits one of three categories. They are either unregenerate (from a biblical perspective), soulish (a more Scriptural term for "flesh,") or spiritual. Everyone is unregenerate until they are born again. We all must start by being born again because we were born in sin. (Romans 3:23) Once people are regenerated they are either soulish or spiritual. Most Believers waiver between soulish and spiritual; sometimes they are soulish and sometimes they are spiritual. Let's take a look at each paradigm.

Unsaved People

Unsaved (unregenerate) people are called "sarkinos" in the Greek. They are dead: fleshly and not spiritual. Whether or not they realize it they operate according to Satan's schematic.

> As for you, *you were dead* in your transgression and sins, in which you used to live when you followed the ways of this world and of the ruler of the kingdom of the air, the spirit who is now at work in those who are disobedient.
> Ephesians 2:1. (Emphasis mine)

God's hope and plan for the unsaved person is that they get saved. He gave His Son as a sacrifice for our sins that we might die to sin and live unto righteousness by whose stripes we are healed.

> We know that the law is spiritual; but I am unspiritual, sold as a slave to sin. Romans 7:14.

Unsaved people cannot hear God. The Gospel is veiled to them so they cannot see the light. (1 Corinthians 4:3-4) And they have little spiritual protection apart from the prayers of others. (2 Corinthians 10:3-5)

Soulish People

Soulish people (from the Greek word "psuchikos") are born again, but are not Spirit-filled. They are saved but not sanctified. They are on their way to heaven but are not living in daily victory. Jesus calls them "lukewarm" in Revelation three. He says He is about to spew them out of His mouth. Their souls are exalted over their human spirits. They have pockets of sin and resistance that keep them from living sanctified lives.

> But the natural (psuchikos) man receiveth not the things of the Spirit of God: for they are foolishness unto him: neither can he know [them], because they are spiritually discerned. 1 Corinthians 2:14 KJV. (note mine)

> So I say, live by the Spirit, and you will not gratify the desires of the sinful nature. For the sinful nature desires what is contrary to the Spirit, and the Spirit what is contrary to the sinful nature. They are in conflict with each other, so that you do not do what you want. . . . Since we live by the Spirit, let us keep in step with the Spirit. Galatians 5:16-17, 25.

> Since we have these promises, dear friends, let us purify ourselves from everything that contaminates body and spirit, *perfecting holiness* out of reverence for God. 2 Corinthians 7:1.

Soulish people seldom hear God speaking. The joy of

the Lordship of Jesus is veiled from them and they have very little spiritual protection. It is a mistake for soulish people to think they will not be tempted beyond what they can bear when they are not following Jesus as Lord.

Spiritual People

Spiritual people (pneumatikos) are regenerate *and* walking in spiritual alignment. A spiritual Christian is one whose human spirit is yielded to the Holy Spirit, whose soul is aligned with their human spirit, and whose body is aligned with their soul.

> Those who live according to the sinful nature have their minds set on what that nature desires; but those who live in accordance with the Spirit have their minds set on what the Spirit desires. The mind of the sinful man is death, but the mind controlled by the Spirit is life and peace.
> Romans 8:5.

Many translators put a capital "S" on the word spirit even when the Bible makes reference to the human spirit rather than the Holy Spirit. Since the Greek language of the New Testament doesn't use capitalization like English does, it is difficult to determine when the Bible is making reference to our human spirits or God's Holy Spirit. I believe many verses like Romans 8:5 and most of those in Galatians chapter five would be better translated with the small "s" on spirit to emphasize the human spirit.

Those who follow their sinful natures have their minds set on that nature. Those who live according to their regenerated human spirits follow what their born again human spirits desire.

Spiritual people know God's voice. Jesus said His

sheep know His voice. (John 10:3-4) Even pre-believers come to Jesus when they sense Him speaking to their hearts but ongoing conversation with the Lord is reserved for truly spiritual people. For them prayer is two-way conversation. They speak *with* the Lord and not just *to* him.

Spiritual people know Jesus as Master and Lord. They obey him because they hear him, love him and trust him to lead them in the way that is best.

Spiritual people have great spiritual protection. (2 Thessalonians 3:3) Rather than being afraid of the devil, the devil is afraid of them!

God designed humans to walk in right alignment with their bodies submitted to their souls, their souls yielded to their human spirits, and their all fully surrendered to God.

We are called to walk in right alignment both within ourselves and with the Lord!

God is more than willing to do His part if we will merely surrender to Him and follow Him.

- "This is the covenant I will make with the house of Israel after that time," declares the LORD. "I will put my law in their minds and write it on their hearts. I will be their God, and they will be my people." Jeremiah 31:33.
- I will give you a new heart and put a new spirit in you; I will remove from you your heart of stone and give you a heart of flesh. And I will put my Spirit in you and move you to follow my decrees and be careful to keep my laws. Ezekiel 36:26-27.

Our part is first of all to surrender fully to God. If we really sang truthfully, many would sing "I surrender some, I surrender some," or "take my life and leave me be." Paul urges us to full surrender:

- Therefore, I urge you, brothers, in view of God's mercy, to offer your bodies as living sacrifices, holy and pleasing to God--this is your spiritual act of worship. Do not conform any longer to the pattern of this world, but be transformed by the renewing of your mind. Then you will be able to test and approve what God's will is--his good, pleasing and perfect will. Romans 12:1-2.

We are responsible to guard our own emotions and attitudes. Stinking thinking has no place in a spiritual person's life.
> Above all else, guard your heart, for it is
> the wellspring of life. Proverbs 4:23.

One of the great mysteries of God is why He gave humans personal sovereignty. While Satan wants to hold people captive to victimization, God wants people to engage their wills. He even leaves people with the choice as to whether or not they will love Jesus and follow him.

One frustration altar counselors face is that people want somebody to fix them while God wants them to engage with him for restoration. Only as they learn to obey God does Jesus manifest to them.
> Whoever has my commands and obeys them, he is the one
> who loves me. He who loves me will be loved by my
> Father, and I too will love him and show myself to him.
> John 14:21.

> It is our responsibility to yield our bodies to the Lord. Spiritual people tell their bodies what to do rather than letting the appetites of bodies take charge. Therefore do not let sin reign in your mortal body so that you obey its evil desires. Do not offer the parts of your body to sin, as instruments of wickedness, but rather offer yourselves to

> God, as those who have been brought from death to life; and offer the parts of your body to him as instruments of righteousness. Romans 6:12-13.

Watchmen Nee rightly said "A spiritual man is not a man born again, but a man born again and walking in alignment." Spiritual alignment brings God's power, presence and authority into a person's life.

When people walk in correct alignment they hear God's voice. They can minister in God's Power and Authority.

> My message and my preaching were not with wise and persuasive words, but with a demonstration of the Spirit's power, so that your faith might not rest on men's wisdom, but on God's power. 1 Corinthians 2:4-5.

You cannot successfully claim God's promises unless you are walking in right spiritual alignment. Rightly aligned people have access to all the promises.

> His divine power has given us everything we need for life and godliness through our knowledge of him who called us by his own glory and goodness. Through these he has given us his very great and precious promises, so that through them you may participate in the divine nature and escape the corruption in the world caused by evil desires. 2 Peter 1:3-4.

I took a class at Shekinah Christian Church in Ann Arbor, Michigan, over a decade ago. It was taught by Brad Bandemer and it changed my life. He taught about right alignment and ended with a prayer of alignment that my wife and I pray in some form nearly every day. I cannot quote it the way Brad taught it, but I share it the way I remember it.

PRAYER OF ALIGNMENT:

In Jesus' Name, I tell my body to submit to my soul.
I tell my soul to submit to my spirit.
I yield my spirit fully to the Holy Spirit.
I ask the Father to fill me with His Holy Spirit.
I choose to walk in the Spirit, and overcome
Satan by the blood of the Lamb
And by the word of my testimony.
And, Holy Spirit, I ask you to show me
every time I slip out of alignment,
that I may realign with you;
spirit, soul, and body.
In Jesus' Name, Amen.

Chapter 15
Power of the Holy Spirit for Right Living

It is true, according to Romans 8:9-15 and 1 Corinthians 1:21-22 that every true Believer has at least a deposit of the Holy Spirit. But as we saw in the last chapter, many believers are soulish rather than truly spiritual.

I personally lived a subnormal Christian life for the first twenty years of my Christian walk even though I was a pastor for 13 of them! I wanted to be spiritual but was bound more to the law than I was to the spirit of liberty in Christ.

I read through the Bible yearly back then (as my wife and I still do) but failed to see the power that was available to those who believe and receive. I skimmed over some weighty passages but never understood them. I want to share a few of them with you and give a bit of my personal testimony. I will start with a familiar verse that I memorized long before its reality manifested in my life.

> Do not get drunk on wine, which leads to debauchery. Instead, be filled with the Spirit. Ephesians 5:18.

I stopped drinking alcohol before I became a Christian but I do remember what a drunk feels like. But I never understood the concept of being "drunk" with the Spirit. I was skeptical when I saw Peter Wagner and Cindy Jacobs lay hands on a minister from another country. They released such an anointing that the man staggered over the platform. I didn't understand it but I knew I needed more power.

To really understand the difference between being drunk with alcohol or with the Spirit it helps to understand the word "debauchery" used in Ephesians 5:18. It is fascinating. In the Greek "debauchery" is a compound word built on "solteria" that means full salvation with an "a - Greek alpha" in front of it that simply means "not". That "a" in front is used like the English "un" in unkind or unborn. Therefore "asolteria" means "unsalvation" or "salvation, not!"

Solteria is the word for full salvation which includes the entire atonement: salvation of spirit, healing of body, restoration of finances, relationships and the like. What Paul is really saying is "Be not drunk with wine which leads to full salvation, healing and restoration--*NOT*, but be filled with the Spirit."

The word translated "filled" describes continual filling to overflowing. If you think of how a good waitress keeps your cup or glass brimming you have a picture of how God wants us to be continually overflowing with the Holy Spirit.

Jesus refers to the Holy Spirit as a good gift from the Father in Luke.

> If you then, though you are evil, know how to give good gifts to your children, how much more will your Father in heaven give the Holy Spirit to those who ask him!"
> Luke 11:13.

I received the gift of salvation by faith in 1972 but I didn't truly receive the "bubbling over" gift of the Holy Spirit until over twenty years later.

I knew the *spring* of the Holy Spirit from salvation but had no understanding of the *river* of the Holy Spirit until after I was baptized in the Holy Spirit.

Jesus said something very interesting to the woman at

the well. She was a Samaritan and needed salvation. They had discussed worship and religion and Jesus knew she was seeking for that which can really satisfy, so he spoke of the spring of living water.

> But whoever drinks the water I give him will never thirst. Indeed, the water I give him will become in him a spring of water welling up to eternal life." John 4:14.

This spring, called "fountain" in some translations, refers to the beginning of salvation. When a person receives the Lord the Holy Spirit begins a good work in them. He is like a spring that refreshes the individual who drinks of it. That is a great start, but the Lord wants to take people deeper. Jesus used the word streams or rivers (depending on translation) to illustrate how God wants the Holy Spirit to flow to and through our lives.

> Whoever believes in me, as the Scripture has said, *streams* of living water will flow from within him." By this he meant the Spirit, whom those who believed in him were later to receive. Up to that time the Spirit had not been given, since Jesus had not yet been glorified.
> John 7:38-39. (emphasis mine)

My Testimony

I never went to church as a boy but was taught to say the Lord's Prayer each night--the one that starts "Now I lay me down to sleep." I did not know God and the only time He became personal to me as a boy was one day when I was so small that my mother was giving me a bath in a sink. I wasn't enjoying it and said "I wish I were dead." She replied, "Well, we can tell God that you want to die."

She called my bluff, but my first real impression of God was a superhuman cop that was ready to kill me if I messed up. It wasn't until years later that I understood the curse of death and suicide that was in my family line.

My parents began dragging me to church when I was in Junior High. It was a liturgical church. At first I enjoyed the atmosphere and learned to respect God. Soon I was asked to be an altar boy and that allowed me to see things from a different perspective. I honored God but didn't know Him.

After a while, an old hen from the congregation took it upon herself to bring me up in the fear and admonition of the Lord. She didn't like the way I carried the cross. She said I carried it all wrong. She also didn't like my fidgeting through the laboriously long 20 or 30 minute messages. After a few weeks of her help I began rebelling against going to church. Usually my parents forced me to go, but I determined that once I grew up that nobody would ever make me go to church again.

When I rejected that church in my heart I also rejected what little I knew about God. I claimed to be an atheist and started to live the wild life as much as I could get away with under the close observation of loving parents. I made fun of the one real Christian I knew. He was the local Baptist preacher who drove my school bus. At Christmas time he gave us gifts of candy bars and pencils which he figured earned him the right to stop the bus and tell us the true Christmas story. I mocked him and claimed I would turn him in to the A.C.L.U. How I wish I could have asked his forgiveness before he went to his reward.

I graduated from high school but was afraid to go to college, so I started working full time at the grocery store where I had worked part time during school. I had a steady girlfriend who was younger than me. Her parents were Christians and faithful to an evangelical church. She was a junior and I had been out of school for less than a year when we discovered she was pregnant. We determined to do the honorable thing and get married. I had been to church with her a few times so we approached the preacher together. He did some good counseling and we were married in his church.

I still didn't think much of church but started going occasionally to keep my wife's family happy. I saw a love in that church that I didn't understand. I met couples who had some good things in their marriages that were missing in mine. I began talking with people at work about the Lord and my hunger grew. Two couples invited us into their homes and both couples had love and warmth far beyond what I had ever experienced. Looking back I can see how God was setting me up according to His blueprint for my life.

At the same time I worked with a man that I did not like. He lacked ambition, was proud and controlling, and always striving for promotion. One day he came to work dejected and I heard his wife had left him. I could understand why, I didn't like him either. But a few weeks later he came walking into the store holding hands with his wife.

He was so changed that he even looked different. I watched him carefully. He began working harder than ever before. His language changed for the better and his voice kinder. Something was changing him from the inside out and I finally asked him about it. He offered to stop by my house with a friend of his and tell me about it. When they came by they simply shared the Four Spiritual Laws and tried to convince me to receive Jesus.

I declined, thinking that I was every bit as good as this new convert. But the seed was planted and I really wanted what he had, so I started doing what he did. I became faithful to church, started reading the Bible daily, tithing my income, and serving as a Sunday School teacher and youth leader.

Everyone was amazed at the change in me, but I knew

it was outward reformation rather than inward transformation. Later I attended a Bill Gothard Basic Youth Conflicts seminar thinking I would be a better youth leader if I took his training.

On Friday night of the seminar Bill explained Romans 10:9-13 in a way that I finally understood. I received Jesus that night and God did a real work in my spirit. I find it interesting, in light of my call to deliverance ministry, that I was born on Halloween and born again at the Masonic Temple in Detroit on March 17, 1972. I was not baptized in the Spirit and my life change was still more reformation than transformation.

Still, I became increasingly involved in serving the Lord. I sensed a call to work with youth. Less than a year later I began full time ministry with Youth for Christ while starting college full time.

After my sophomore year of college I took our youth group on a mission trip to the Carolinas that was headed up by a neat old preacher. My son was three years old and life was good. But every night as the preacher spoke I sensed I was being called to preach. That was the furthest thing from my imagination or desire. I thought preachers were boring! I wanted to work with young people and help shape them to shape a nation.

I was also terribly self-conscious and afraid to speak in public. But on the final night of the crusade I knew that I either had to surrender to God's call to preach or deliberately disobey Him. I went to the altar and surrendered to preach. I wept, not because I was happy but because I was broken at the thought of giving in to God's plan for my life that was so different than my own.

An amazing thing happened after I surrendered. God put the desire in my heart to preach! The pastor who led the trip to the Carolinas told me he wanted to hire me after my third year of college, to replace his assistant who planned on moving on to Seminary. I based everything on that prospect. I figured I didn't need to move our growing family from our small home with two bedrooms. I figured our worn out roof could wait.

Since I would have special discounts from Spring Arbor College if I became an assistant pastor, I used up most of my financial aid. I didn't think I had to worry anymore about the requirement to finish my college work by doing a twenty hour a week internship in something other than Youth for Christ.

But the bottom fell out the next spring. The assistant pastor who was supposed to leave for seminary decided to put it off for a year. There was no way I could afford to move into a bigger home or even reroof our old home. I couldn't possibly work 20 extra hours a week as an intern to complete my degree while working full time for YFC, rearing a family and taking a full load at college. Without the grant I counted on from being an assistant pastor, it didn't seem possible to even finish college. On one particular June day this all weighed so heavy on me that I threw my hands up in despair. It was warm and I was working in my garden--turning over the obstacles in my head more than I was the soil. I finally looked up to heaven and desperately cried "I give up!"

I went in for a glass of ice tea and sat down with the prospect of just sitting there, without any hope or thought of how to make anything work out. My prospects were all shattered and I had no hope.

Shortly after I released this all into God's hands the conference superintendent of my denomination called. Some of my professors had recommended me as a prospective pastor. He said he needed an answer right away and wanted to drive to Sturgis and interview me.

He came and I was soon invited and appointed to pastor my first church. I am still amazed how God, within three hours of casting my cares upon him, made it possible for me to finish college with great financial aid. He moved me 20 miles closer to school and into a lovely three bedroom home. My income increased enough that we could take care of things that had seemed out of reach.

When I agreed to take that first church my wife wasn't very happy. She said, "You don't know how to preach." Looking back, she was right about my inability to preach. My early sermons were written like term papers, well studied but with very little inspiration or anointing.

But every church I took grew and many were saved through our ministry. But something was missing. I had a fairly accurate grasp of Scriptures and learned the form of religion well, but I lacked power for living and for ministry.

Few would argue that my life was reformed. The old habits were gone and better habits were formed. But I still lacked the true inner transformation that was needed for me to be everything God wanted me to be as a man, a husband, a father and a preacher.

I was deeply hurt a few years later over a Christian School we started. We knew it was God's will to launch a Christian school that would keep biblical morality within the context of excellent education.

Our school children were scoring far higher on the California Achievement Tests than the local public school students, but one Christian School in our conference didn't approve of the way we were training children apart from state certified teachers, curriculum and buildings.

I was called to a special meeting over this issue. As I

drove to a special meeting where our school would be scrutinized I knew in my heart that if the conference required me to close the school or hire state certified teachers, or use state certified curriculum or hold our building to state standards for large schools, that I was to resign.

The conference decided to make an example of me and forbid me to continue running the school unless we started using state approved teachers, curriculum and the like.

I was convicted to obey God rather than man and resigned. What followed was ugly and in my disillusionment I turned toward extreme fundamentalists for instruction and fellowship.

They taught me to despise any talk about the gifts of the Spirit, being baptized with the Spirit, divine healing, prophecy and the like. I pulled away from the local ministerial association because some of the ministers were labeled "liberal" by my new peers.

As my pride grew I also stopped fellowshipping with any that didn't use the KJV Bible, enforce "godly" standards of dress and music, or think the way I was taught to think.

I became hardened and proud and that pride led to my fall. It was 27 years ago as of this writing that my first wife left and we divorced. Of course I blamed her at first, but looking back I think I would have left me too!

Being a concrete (hard and set in my ways) fundamentalist, I didn't think God could ever use me again. I resigned my church, sold my library and began searching for freedom and happiness in all the wrong ways.

I never stopped going to church. I actually visited 26 churches over the next three years trying to find one where I might receive the love, acceptance and forgiveness that I desperately needed. Unfortunately, all but a couple of them treated me the same way I had previously treated Christians who fell into sin or divorced.

I became a home supervisor for developmentally disabled adults. Those precious people taught me more about human nature than all the classes I had taken. It was the easiest and highest paying job I'd ever had but I wasn't happy. Being a preacher wasn't something I did--it is who I am.

I was blessed by an opportunity to preach in a county jail in 1988. The first invitation led to another until I became the "second Monday of the month" jail preacher. I continue doing that to this day and thank God for the original chaplain who believed in me when I didn't believe in myself and gave me a chance when I didn't deserve one.

The year 1990 was a turning point for me. I was miserable, working a good job but one I was not called to. I hated being a single parent but had no healthy relationships. I was bound by a fear of rejection and the need to belong to someone and have them belong to me. Love hunger led me to do things that I never thought I would do.

I had no understanding of deliverance or deep healing, but I did know the value of full surrender. I finally threw my hands up again and told the Lord that if He wanted me to remain single until I died and never wanted me to enter the ministry again, that I would still yield fully to his ways.

After searching for love, acceptance and forgiveness in 25 different churches, I finally tried one that was pastored by Jack and Cathy Eitelbus. They understood one thing that I had never understood: grace. They loved me, accepted me, challenged me, and fed me good spiritual food. Two years later they helped me back into the ministry in a church in Sturgis, Michigan.

I loved being back in the ministry. I was finally able to again be and do what God created me to be and do. I determined to do things differently this time. I wanted to pastor a church of the second, and third, and fourth chance.

I wanted to help people get back on their feet with the Lord's help. After five years out of the ministry I was ordained in a holiness church. I thought I had arrived, for the history of that denomination was full of powerful truths about the Holy Spirit, the Kingdom of God, healing and deliverance.

My goals were right and are still being fulfilled. But I still knew more about reformation than I did about transformation. Things went great at first. We grew rapidly, but I still had inner struggles and knew there had to be more.

Sixteen months after taking the pastorate in Sturgis I was blessed with the gift of a second chance at marriage. I married a woman who fully became my helpmate in life and ministry. The only problem I saw was she claimed that God actually talked with her! She even sought his approval before she agreed to marry me! Even though I didn't believe (back then) that God still talked to people, I earnestly prayed that she would hear Him say "yes." And she did. Pamela became my wife on December 12, 1993.

I saw things in her that I had never seen in Christians before. She had a peace that passes understanding and the things God revealed to her were beyond human imagination.

Even though I had been dogmatically fundamentalist, I started seeking the Lord for His voice and His will. He began showing me things that ran contrary to the form of religion I was used to and I increasingly became open to the things of the Spirit.

The Holy Spirit showed me that what we called worship was simply singing songs and enjoying four part harmony. He showed me that what we called church was more like a club. He showed me that doing church as usual was devoid of the power and effectiveness seen in the churches in the New Testament. I began making changes that were not at all popular to religious people.

About this time I took part in a Pastors' Prayer Summit where we spent a few days at a retreat center. During a time alone in the woods it began to rain and I sought refuge in a huge hollow tree. As I sat there God began to speak and I recorded what He was saying. I don't have that journal anymore, but I remember him saying that institutional Christianity was like that tree. It was big and beautiful on the outside but dead and decaying on the inside. He revealed that many things done in the name of Jesus and His church are but a form of religion that denies the power of God.

I didn't think much of it at the time, but I was still in a seeking mode. I was led to go on a 40-day fast called by Bill Bright. I read his book about the coming revival and lived on water and (at the insistence of my doctor) a daily protein shake made with water. Still nothing seemed to happen. I lost 40 pounds in forty days and a rumor started that I had cancer, but other than that it was life and ministry as usual.

Shortly after that time, however, I was strongly impressed to go back to school for my Masters and Doctorate. I saw an ad for the Wagner Leadership Institute, W.L.I. It was sponsored by an apostolic tribe of Christianity I had never heard of.

The school was apostolic and I thought all the apostles had died after the first century A.D. I didn't know where I would find the money to attend, or even if I had what it takes to go back to college 23 years after graduating from Spring Arbor College. But I sensed God wanted me to go, and so started a whole new journey.

I had already begun operating in the authority delegated by Christ to his followers. We were doing some deliverance according to an evangelical pattern. Some of the sick people we prayed for were actually healed. My wife heard God on a regular basis. I had begun a daily listening room and was far more proficient at hearing and recording God's voice than ever before. But I sure wasn't prepared for what was ahead.

My very first series of classes concluded with the National School of the Prophets. That stretched me far beyond my religious wineskins. To be honest, I was so skeptical that I missed much of it, but was so shocked by the awe of it that I couldn't quit going. I continued attending and completed my schooling with proficiencies in deliverance and intercession.

During the National School of the Prophets I introduced myself to Barbara Yoder after she spoke one afternoon. She told me to call her office for an appointment and she graciously met with me and invited me to be a part of a group that later became Breakthrough Apostolic Ministries Network.

I began attending meetings where people prayed until they entered the Council of the Lord. I was amazed at how things operated from relationship rather than religion. The Holy Spirit orchestrated those meetings and used his gifts to release strategies to advance the Kingdom.

Later, at another W.L.I. large training event, Tommy Tenney spoke. The speakers before him spoke with confidence that I misread as arrogance. But Tommy spoke with such great humility that when he stepped onto the platform God joined him. I had never experienced God in such a tangible way. I could actually smell him; it was the deepest and richest smell of spikenard I've ever experienced, and it filled the room.

When Tommy gave the altar call I threw off my resistance and reluctance, and ran to the altar where Tommi Femrite prayed for me. She didn't know me from Adam but she spoke into my life in a way that I knew had to be God.

She said that I had been pouring out my whole ministry and that it was time that I allowed God to pour in. She told me to open wide my mouth and God would fill it.

I did as instructed and sucked in all of God I could possibly hold. The Holy Spirit, ever a gentleman, didn't release any great manifestations to or through me that day but something changed inside that was far more than flesh driven reformation. Actual transformation began accelerating in me. The spring of the Spirit became a river flowing from my belly.

Several weeks later I was enjoying my monthly fast day at the same retreat center where I had taken refuge in the hollow tree. That day, when I got to that tree, it had blown over. God began speaking about how dead institutional churchianity was falling, and I began rejoicing. That same week news reports began about sexual abuse that had been covered up for years in one particular religious system. It took me years to realize that when God told me that dead institutional Christianity was falling, that He was talking to me, *about me* -- not about the denominational church like I previously thought.

After being a victim of forms of religion that denied the power of God for several years, I was ready for every form of religion that denied the power of God to break off my life.

I stood before the fallen tree and suddenly began grieving for all those caught up in institutional Christianity who believed they are heaven-bound because they have been baptized or are on a church roll. I began weeping for the lost who think they are saved within the vestiges of *church as usual*. My weeping increased in intensity and suddenly, without warning, I began praying in tongues! Mind you, I had taught against tongues for years. I was such a mixture of the old and the new wineskins that my first response was "If this is of the devil, stop it, NOW, in Jesus' Name!!"

Well it didn't stop for 90 minutes, so I asked the Lord to let me know what I was praying and he released the gift of interpretation.

I had been on the outskirts of the River for some time. The fountain had increased and was flowing some. But that day I was dunked, baptized, immersed, and filled with the Holy Spirit in a way that I didn't know was possible.

Life didn't get easier, it got harder. People that I had loved, many whom I had brought to Jesus and taught to be religious rose up against me. My denomination rose up and made me go through a probationary period where they examined my life and doctrines. After six months, I was told that my record was clean and they found no fault in me. By that time our elders found fault with the group we had been part of, so we made the difficult decision to leave and become independent.

Whenever there is a new move of God there seems to be extremes and I admit that happened to me. I tried to push others into what I was experiencing before they were ready. But the pendulum has swung back to a new normal that allows Holy Spirit His way.

Every step that I've taken with the Lord has been a step up, even though some of them hit the basement for a while. The most important step that I've taken, apart from my initial salvation, was to believe the Father for and receive the gift of the Holy Spirit. May that river of the Holy Spirit well up and overflow for you and for me!

Chapter 16
In His SOVEREIGN Image

> ❧ So God created man in his own image, in the image of God he created him; male and female he created them. Genesis 1:27.

Several chapters ago I shared how the earth had become void and without form.

> ❧ Now the earth was {Or possibly became} formless and empty, darkness was over the surface of the deep, and the Spirit of God was hovering over the waters. Genesis 1:2.

In our first look at Genesis we saw that "in the Beginning" referred not only to the beginning of the earth as we know it, but also to the beginning of God's redemptive plan for the earth. Somehow, probably after the fall of Lucifer, the earth had become empty, void, chaotic and dark. But the Spirit of God was brooding over the earth wanting it to come into the fullness of God's destiny. In like manner the Holy Spirit continues to brood over places of chaos that He might bring Kingdom order.

Part One: God's plan was to create Kingdom order in the earth. Therefore He created all things in six days and set the times and seasons in place according to His own good and perfect will.

Part Two: Part two of God's schematic was to delegate authority to humans to maintain, extend and expand Kingdom order in the earth.

God created humans--male and female--to have and enjoy life more abundantly and to extend Kingdom rule upon the earth. Satan's chief interest in people is to kill, steal and destroy God's image, glory and likeness from them. That is why he tempts people to sin. Since God never sins, it destroys His likeness and glory in us when we do sin.

Satan Schemes to Steal Human Control

When we sin we fall short of the glory of God and therefore we fall short of His sovereign image. That makes us lose control and become pawns of Satan rather than partners with God in Kingdom rule.

When we lose God's sovereign image we lose grasp of His destiny (another way of saying schematic) for our lives. We fall out of God's intended abundance, and into Satan's trap of loss, destruction, and chaos that keeps us from advancing the Kingdom in our own lives and world.

God is making this clearer to His Church. God created humans to take charge of the environment in a Kingdom way, to extend His rule throughout the earth and thus forcefully advance the Kingdom of God.

Satan wants to usurp control from us so we will succumb to his pressure and allow darkness and chaos to reign. He tempts us to give in to the spirit of victimization, rather than standing and ruling as victorious ones in Christ Jesus!

Restoring Abundance and Order

A major key to restoring abundance and order is regaining the likeness of God's sovereignty in our lives. We must do that in order to advance the Kingdom of God.

Satan wants to usurp human authority so we will be pawns and peons, rather than partners with God. Satan has infiltrated our theology with all sorts of unbiblical lies that we accept as truth.

A few lies that deny human sovereignty:

1) "When my number is up I will die."
Even though the Bible says that we can extend our lives simply by obeying our parents (Ephesians 6:1-3), Satan wants us to roll over and play dead, as if there is nothing we can do about our longevity. I've read reports that four years after people stop smoking their health will be as if they had never smoked, but people who believe they will die when their number is up, lose motivation to take advantage of things that will lengthen their lives.

I had the painful duty of conducting the funeral service of a young man who died in a drunken crash with one of his best friends. His family had never been active in church but they sounded very religious at the funeral home. I heard them comforting each other with words like "God knows best," "he's in a better place now," "now he is one of God's angels," or "it was his time to go."

They seemed to believe God's plan for this young man's life included driving drunk and crashing into a tree at a high rate of speed. That wasn't God's blueprint for this precious boy's life. Jesus came that he might have life more abundantly. It's always Satan scheme to kill, steal and destroy.

> Whoever of you loves life and desires to see many (versus few) good days, keep your tongue from evil and your lips from speaking lies. Turn from evil and do good; seek

peace and pursue it. Psalm 34:12-14. (note mine)

2) "Everything that happens is God's will."

God is not the author of evil. It is never His will for people to be raped, molested, poor, hungry, tormented and the like. It is not God's will for babies to be born with AIDS because of their parent's promiscuity. God doesn't will for people to die early deaths because they eat too much junk food, won't exercise, smoke, drink or do drugs.

I ministered to a young man who had cancer of the knee. Both he and his mother received the Lord the first time I met with them. The young man was scheduled to have his knee amputated, but after prayer that was not needed.

For a while the young man and his mother were faithful to the Lord and to the church but soon began to fall away. His cancer came back and we prayed and it went into remission again and they came back to the Lord.

Then they fell away again and returned to their previous lifestyles. Several years later I was called upon because the boy, then a young man, was near death and in excruciating pain. They asked me to visit them, so after a season of prayer I did. The Lord had told me that I could pray for the pain to leave but I was not to pray for his healing.

I explained that when I arrived. The man was in such pain that I offered to pray right away. After prayer he stood up, walked around the room without pain and exclaimed that he had not been able to do that for months. When he sat back down I called him to repentance. Several in the room joined in the prayer.

The Lord had highlighted a severe truth to me that day before I visited them and I knew I was to share it.

"Your own conduct and actions have brought this upon you. This is your punishment. How bitter it is! How it pierces to the heart!" Jeremiah 4:18.

I explained that God was even more concerned about his soul than he was about his body. I encouraged full repentance and suggested that God might be merciful if they cried out to him.

After talking for a short while he asked if it was OK if he continued smoking medical marijuana for pain. So I asked, "Are you in any pain now?" He said "No, I haven't had pain since you prayed." So I asked, "Who took away your pain" and he answered "Jesus." So I asked "Why would you turn back to medical marijuana when you just experienced the touch of God?" Unfortunately he put his trust in marijuana rather than the Lord.

He died a few days later. My heart was grieved for that young man and his family but I am convinced that his early death was not God's will.

3) "It doesn't matter how hard you try —stuff happens."

Do not be deceived: God cannot be mocked. A man reaps what he sows. Galatians 6:7.

Satan wants us to believe that "whatever will be, will be" so we might as well give in to whatever is, and simply roll with the punches. But God created us to extend His rule, not give into the ruler of this age.

Man's sovereign image has fallen short of God's image. A major key for restoring personal abundance is to restore God's sovereign image in our lives so we can advance the Kingdom of God.

Think of the Lord's Prayer: "… Thy Kingdom come… thy will be done on earth as it is in heaven!" Who has the responsibility for praying that Kingdom order be restored and maintained on earth?

Jesus told His disciples "this then is how YOU should pray." God's understanding of man's authority is so great that He requires people to pray for His Kingdom to come and His will to be done!

God gave 5 major commands in Genesis 1:28 and amplifies them in the New Testament. People have violated each of these commands. You have to hand it to humans--at least they are consistent. Violation to these commands has negative effects on marriages, families, church, government, and the market place.

I preached a sermon way back in 1976 that I still remember to this day. The title was "Who is they?" They are ruining our schools; they are ruining our church, our families, our children and our marriages. They are ruining our job market, they are ruining our city, and they are destroying our nation. Who is they? We can point our finger at the world, but it is time to realize that when we do that, we have 3 fingers pointing back at us. Who is they? We are they. I am they. You are they.

Only Kingdom people can restore order so things will be the way God designed for our blessing. Look at Genesis 1:28.

\ God blessed them and said to them, "Be <u>fruitful</u> and <u>increase</u> in number; <u>fill</u> the earth and <u>subdue</u> it. <u>Rule</u> over the fish of the sea and the birds of the air and over every living creature that moves on the ground."
Genesis 1:28. (Emphasis mine)

The Sins of Omission

The first sin of omission is "Be Fruitful."
The word translated fruitful here is also translated

increased, grow, bring fruit, make fruitful and carries the idea of reproducing after one's kind. Kingdom people are to reproduce Kingdom people. Each one of the commands given in Genesis 1:28 has a New Testament fulfillment.

A New Testament amplification of *be fruitful*:

> I am the vine; you are the branches. If a man remains in me and I in him, he will bear much fruit; apart from me you can do nothing. 8 This is to my Father's glory, that you bear much fruit, showing yourselves to be my disciples. 16 You did not choose me, but I chose you and appointed you to go and bear fruit--fruit that will last. Then the Father will give you whatever you ask in my name.
> John 15:5, 8, 16.

This speaks to reproducing ourselves physically and spiritually. God is not into zero population growth regarding physical children or spiritual children.

The second sin of omission is "multiply."

The word here is also translated: increase, much, many, more, exceedingly, and abundance. Christians are to become great, be or become many, be or become much, be or become numerous. If God wants any church members, He wants more church members.

Two New Testament amplifications to multiply:

> Then Jesus came to them and said, "All authority in heaven and on earth has been given to me. Therefore go and make disciples of all nations, baptizing them in the name of the Father and of the Son and of the Holy Spirit, and teaching them to obey everything I have commanded you. And surely I am with you to the end of the age.
> Matthew 28:18-20.

> And the things you have heard me say in the presence of many witnesses entrust to reliable men who will also be qualified to teach others. 2 Timothy 2:2.

The third sin of omission is: "Fill the earth."

The word for *fill* is translated: fill, 107 times, full, 48 times, fulfill, 28 times, etc. The definitions include "to fill, be full; fullness, abundance; to consecrate, fill the land; to be filled, be armed, and be satisfied."

A New Testament amplification of fill the earth:
> He who descended is the very one who ascended higher than all the heavens, *in order to fill the whole universe.* It was he who gave some to be apostles, some to be prophets, some to be evangelists, and some to be pastors and teachers, to prepare God's people for works of service, so that the body of Christ may be built up until we all reach unity in the faith and in the knowledge of the Son of God and become mature, attaining to the whole measure of the fullness of Christ. Ephesians 4:10-13. (emphasis mine)

The Lord purposes for His Apostolic Church to fill the whole universe with His Glory and Likeness. It's time to step up to the line and go to work!

The fourth sin of omission is "Subdue or dominate the earth."

The word translated "subdue" here is also translated *bring into subjection, bring into bondage, keep under and force.* Its definitions include: 1) to subject, subdue, force, keep under, and bring into bondage; 1a1) make subservient; 1a3) to subdue, dominate and tread down.

We sin against a Most Holy God when we sit back and

let the powers of darkness overcome our lives, families and the land! We are charged by King Jesus to extend the Kingdom of Heaven's rule over the earth. We are to bring the world under our control, rather than coming under the world's control!

The way the Kingdom of God advances against the kingdom of darkness is that Kingdom people begin to subdue the earth and take dominion back for God! That is how we regain His sovereign image!

A New Testament amplification of subduing and dominating the earth:
\ I tell you the truth: Among those born of women there has not risen anyone greater than John the Baptist; yet he who is least (have you ever felt "less than"?) in the kingdom of heaven is greater than he. From the days of John the Baptist until now, the kingdom of heaven has been forcefully advancing, and forceful men *lay hold* of it. Matthew 11:11-12. (note and emphasis mine)

The fifth sin of omission is "rule."

This word is translated: rule, dominion, prevaileth, reign, and ruler. Listen to its meaning: 1) to rule, have dominion, dominate, and tread down; 1a) to have dominion, rule, subjugate; to cause to dominate.

There is no way that God wants Believers to throw up their hands and let a bunch of lazy sponges occupy Wall Street, or allow pinheads to outlaw Prayer from City public meetings, or allow drug and alcohol abuse to ruin our cities. God commands us to subdue these things -- but be subject to them!

New Testament amplifications of ruling:
\ And from Jesus Christ, [who is] the faithful witness, [and] the first begotten of the dead, and the prince of the kings of

the earth. Unto him that loved us, and washed us from our sins in his own blood, and hath made us kings and priests, unto God and his Father; to him [be] glory and dominion for ever and ever. Amen. Revelation 1:5-6.

↳ And they sang a new song: "You are worthy to take the scroll and to open its seals, because you were slain, and with your blood you purchased men for God from every tribe and language and people and nation. You have made them to be a kingdom and priests to serve our God, and they will reign on the earth." Revelation 5:9-10.

As we debunk the lies concerning human sovereignty and repent of the sins of omission, we will be able to move into divine supply to accomplish Kingdom purposes.

Principles for advancing the Kingdom
The Principle of Supply

Hudson Taylor, Missionary to China, said "God's work done God's way will never lack for God's supply." It was so from the very beginning. That is something this church needs to consider--are we doing God's work in such a way that He wants to supply our needs?

↳ Then God said, "I give you every seed-bearing plant on the face of the whole earth and every tree that has fruit with seed in it. They will be yours for food. 30 And to all the beasts of the earth and all the birds of the air and all the creatures that move on the ground--everything that has the breath of life in it--I give every green plant for food."
And it was so. Genesis 1:29-30.

People have memorized and taken Philippians 4:13 and 4:19 out of context.

↳ I can do everything through him who gives me strength.

> Philippians 4:13.
>
> ✝ And my God will meet all your needs according to his glorious riches in Christ Jesus. Philippians 4:19.

We love to stand on the promises of divine strength and provision, but we seem to miss the surrounding verses that say Paul knew what it was like to be in plenty and in need, well fed and hungry, in troubles and the like.

The Principle of Work

> ✝ The LORD God took the man and put him in the Garden of Eden to work it and take care of it. Genesis 2:15.

God's design is for work to be rewarding and fulfilling. Satan's tries to program us and make us think work is something to be avoided. God wants people to do whatever they do for His glory but Satan presents a false dualism that perceives some things as sacred and others secular. When people buy into that, they fail to take God with them into their careers and be game changers.

Work really isn't a naughty four-letter word. God created work *before* man sinned. When we get to Genesis 3 we will see how sin brought greater resistance to the good work God intends for people to do--but the principle of work is that we partner with God to execute Kingdom will on earth as it is in heaven.

Do you remember the fourth commandment? Most people reduce it to "remember the Sabbath." But there is more to it than that.

> ✝ Six days <u>you shall labor and do all your work</u>, but the seventh day is a Sabbath to the LORD your God. Exodus 20:9-10a. (emphasis mine)

God told people to labor and do all their work. He put a Sabbath restriction on work because people tend to get so caught up in their work that they forget to rest, renew and re-create in the Lord.

It is WORK to advance the Kingdom of God. It takes forceful hard-working people to walk in sovereign authority to make things the way God wants them to be, rather than accepting things as they are.

When God created man, He gave him dominion over the animals, the birds of the air, and the fish of the sea. He told man to tend the earth and take care of it. God wanted people to be stewards of the earth for God. But Satan usurped his authority to become ruler of the earth. In Christ we take it back!

My interest is always sparked when I see the New Testament revise an Old Testament quote. For example: Isaiah 53:5 says "with his stripes we *are* healed" and 1 Peter 2:24 says "by whose stripes ye *were* healed." The first looks forward to the cross, and the second looks back to the cross. Psalm 68 and Ephesians 4 are full of such comparisons but we will only refer to two of them.

> When you ascended on high, you led captives in your train; you *received* gifts from men, even from the rebellious-- that you, O LORD God, might dwell there. Psalm 68:18. (emphasis mine)

> This is why it says: "When he ascended on high, he led captives in his train and *gave* gifts to men." Ephesians 4:8. (emphasis mine)

I wrestled with the "misquoting" of David's "received" to Paul's "gave". Why would Paul write "gave," when it is obvious he is referring back to David's scripture?

The context of Psalm 68 and Ephesians 4 both include the picture of God dwelling on earth through men. But there is a huge difference between the word *received* gifts in Psalm 68 and the word *gave* gifts in Ephesians Chapter 4. In Psalm 68:18 Jesus received gifts, even from the rebellious. In Ephesians, Jesus gives those gifts to His apostolic church.

Whenever I have a problem understanding scripture I try to go to the author. So I asked the Lord why He used "received" in Psalms and "gave" in Ephesians. I sensed it was Jesus who answered.

He said, "When I died, I entered the lower earthly regions and commanded the devil and rebellious humans to give back the dominion, authority, anointing, responsibility and personal sovereignty they usurped through human sin."

In essence, Jesus took back what the devil had stolen from sinful and rebellious humans. Then He said, "After my resurrection I released all these things back to my apostolic people."

The target result in both Psalm 68 and Ephesians 4 is the same as God's original plan for humans in Genesis--that they be fruitful, multiply, rule and subdue the earth and fill it with heaven's rule!

That is why Jesus could prophesy, "All authority in heaven and on earth has been given to me-therefore go...." That is why we need to pray before God works. He has delegated His authority to us over the earth realm.

Think of how God sought for a man to stand in the gap so He wouldn't have to destroy the land. We cannot really understand Ezekiel 23:30 apart from the verse that follows.

> "I looked for a man among them who would build up the wall and stand before me in the gap on behalf of the land

so I would not have to destroy it, but I found none. So I will pour out my wrath on them and consume them with my fiery anger, bringing down on their own heads all they have done, declares the Sovereign LORD."
Ezekiel 23:30, followed by 23:31.

God so fully delegated His authority and dominion over the earth to man that He needed a human being to exercise the imputed authority God released to mankind. When God couldn't find a person to stand in the gap on behalf of the land, He had to destroy it!

As we ask God to restore His sovereign image in us, we will be able to restore His divine order (absence of chaos) in our lives and world. That is God's schematic for humans and for the advancement of His Kingdom on earth. That is the opposite of Satan's schematic. Humans are the deciding factor here. We do have rule, authority and dominion, especially since Jesus took these gifts back from the rebellious and granted them to His apostolic kingdom people!

Chapter 17
Parable of a Laptop with a Forgotten Cord

God designed people to operate in His kairos (opportune) timing. He wants to lead people to keep in step with the Spirit by doing *what* He is doing, *when* He is doing it! But Satan wants chronological time to control people. Consider the following Scriptures.

> ⸙ You know the truth—let your life show it! Live life, then, with a due sense of responsibility, not as men who do not know the meaning and purpose of life but as those who do. *Make the best use of your time, despite all the difficulties of these days. Don't be vague but firmly grasp what you know to be the will of God.* Don't get your stimulus from wine for there is always the danger of excessive drinking, but let the Spirit stimulate your souls. Express your joy in singing among yourselves psalms and hymns and spiritual songs, making music in your hearts for the ears of God! Thank God at all times for everything, in the name of our Lord Jesus Christ. And "fit in with" each other, because of your common reverence for Christ. Ephesians 5:15-21 Phillips. (emphasis mine)

> ⸙ Redeeming the *time*, because the days are evil. For this reason be not foolish, but understanding what [is] the will of the Lord. And be not drunk with wine, in which is *debauchery; but be filled with the Spirit.*

Ephesians 5:16-18 Darby. (emphasis mine)

Don't waste your time on useless work, mere busywork, the barren pursuits of darkness. Expose these things for the sham they are. It's a scandal when people waste their lives on things they must do in the darkness where no one will see. Rip the cover off those frauds and see how attractive they look in the light of Christ.
Wake up from your sleep,
Climb out of your coffins;
Christ will show you the light!
So watch your step. Use your head. Make the most of every chance you get. These are desperate times! Don't live carelessly, unthinkingly. Make sure you understand what the Master wants. Don't drink too much wine. That cheapens your life. Drink the Spirit of God, huge draughts of him. Sing hymns instead of drinking songs! Sing songs from your heart to Christ. Sing praises over everything, any excuse for a song to God the Father in the name of our Master, Jesus Christ. Ephesians 5:11-20 MSG.

Do you ever get so busy and distracted that you forget important things? I did that on a fast day. My prayer partner Scott and I had prayer-walked early, then I hurried through my prayer list so I could get to Amigo Centre by 8:00. Scott kept hearing the word "time" and urged me to ask the Lord about time. So I hurried out to Amigo, set up my computer and then discovered I forgot my power cord and only had a couple hours of battery left. I sat down and the Lord started releasing lessons concerning both His and the devil's schematics concerning time.

Throughout this section I will use italics for what I sensed the Lord saying and regular print for the rest.

Lesson 1: Time is flying and accelerating.

I sat down, turned the computer on and said "Father, Scott told me to ask you about TIME." *Douglas, your computer battery is a parable about time. You only have a certain amount of time left to accomplish what I want you to do. <u>You have adequate time, but limited time</u>. I am not prophesying an early death for you will live to a good old age; but I am pointing out that time is going by much faster than you realize. For most people time seems to accelerate as they approach their senior years and you are fast approaching those years.*

Lesson 2: God's priorities trump downsizing or working less.

Therefore it is urgent that you follow my priorities for your life. That has a lot more to do about how you use your time than it does about the idea of downsizing. You could buy time by selling your house, buying a smaller property and giving up your huge garden but that is not my will for the immediate future. (We have time to use – not to waste)

Somehow we need to move beyond the American Dream of retiring early and squandering our twilight years playing or traveling. I can't find many examples in the Scripture where God told people to retire--can you? But I admire those who take on new assignments in their 80's and 90's.

Lesson 3: Don't limit others by doing it all yourself.

You can also buy time by further delegating the work that you do, which others can do as well or better. You can ask for and receive a secretary. You can fully turn the Council over to its members and spend very little time in training another to carry it. You can open the pulpit up on a more regular basis. You can ask young and old, male and female to give messages.

People grow through experience and they receive experience by having opportunities. I've known for some time that my wife and I need to prepare to pass the baton. The best way to do that is gradually, and with thorough training that shows people what to do and how to do it, and then help them start doing it.

Lesson 4: We need to discern the greater works God has for each one.

> For it is by grace you have been saved, through faith—and this is not from yourselves, it is the gift of God— not by works, so that no one can boast. For we are God's handiwork, created in Christ Jesus to do good works, which God prepared in advance for us to do.
> Ephesians 2:8-10. (emphasis mine)

I sensed the Lord saying, *"Remain in me and it will be MY work that is done through you!"* God has a prophetic destiny for each person. Therefore, it is important that we discover it so we can do what we were created to do.

> Now God has us where he wants us, with all the time in this world and the next to shower grace and kindness upon us in Christ Jesus. Saving mankind is all his idea, and all his work. All we do is trust him enough to let him do it. It's God's gift from start to finish! We don't play the major role. If we did, we'd probably go around bragging that we'd done the whole thing! No, we neither make nor save ourselves. God does both the making and saving. He invites each of us through Christ Jesus to join him in the work he does, the good work he has gotten ready for us to do, we had better work! Ephesians 2:7-10 MSG

Wow the Message can make old truths come alive!

Lesson 5: Busyness is not the key---doing the right thing is.

You are busy all the time and most of what you do is important – it is just not for you to do. The Church grows as each member does its work and as you begin to release things to others, even little things like power points and bulletins. Many will be used, feel important and accept an ownership for the church that they do not currently have. You can trust me with your people and MY church.

John Maxwell said "It isn't how hard we swing the axe that matters. What really matters is how high the wood pile grows." One principle behind the Apostle Paul's success was his focus. Again, as Maxell put it "This one thing I do, not these many things I dabble in."

**Lesson 6: Don't be tricked into taking
a break when you need rest.**

The Lord said: *you have considered adding an evening devotional time since the first of the year but have not fully entered it. You are so tired at night that you let your body run the show rather than moving in the Spirit through your human spirit to do my total will. It is time for that to change. You do have a need for rest, but greater rest comes through spiritual activity than watching television or reading the news.*

I've done well following the Lord's lead in doing devotions every morning and my daily listening room almost every night. But I am often so tired by evening that I think I deserve a break today and fail to do what brings true rest and restoration to my soul. I've been guilty of letting my body tell my spirit what to do rather than vice versa. But when I follow God's ways and timing, things go much better.

Lesson 7: Greatest effectiveness and least weariness come

from letting Jesus be the Lord of your schedule.

John Maxwell has a way of saying profound things in simple ways. I once heard him say "you are always somewhere doing something." He is right, but it is too easy to be in the right place doing an important thing rather than the most important thing. People are important--nearly as important as God. But I've had to limit my time on Email and severely limit time on Facebook because such time can be squandered on trivial stuff rather than true relationships.

Lesson 8: We don't have enough time to ignore Warnings.

God gave still another valuable lesson from my computer when I nearly lost everything I had recorded. He said, *"You nearly lost everything I spoke this morning because you tried to do a "save as" from rich text to Word and ignored the warning that came up before you saved. Therefore you had to do extra work searching for and "redeeming" the text of my earlier words.*

It is vitally important that you follow the little warning signs that I send your way--especially those that come through prophetic counsel. In so doing none of your work will be lost, and you will not have to scramble to get back on course.

My older sister blew up her 1965 Volkswagen Beetle because she didn't think she had time to call for help when her oil light came on. She lost a lot of time by ignoring the warning. Our church has lost a lot of time, because it has ignored warnings.

There've been times when I placed people in leadership when others have shared the red flags they sensed. Every time I ignored their flags it cost me time, money and growth in the end.

Lesson 9: We need to order our time rather

than allow it to control us.

As my time at Amigo drew to a close I simply asked, "Father?" Knowing how low my battery was He said, *"Douglas, save quickly and save often as we talk."* I'm glad I obeyed because the computer suddenly shut down a few minutes later.

God said: *I have shown you many things this day, not the least of which is how you need to view and ORDER time rather than letting time order you. What I have shown you about time is not just for you. Each person in the Body has a prophetic destiny and many don't even realize it because time is running them rather than vice versa. I have shared with you the truth about "redeeming the time" or "buying up the opportunity" because the days are evil today.*

Lesson 10: Don't lose sight of the main thing in the shuffle of the many.

God shared: *Part of the evil of these days is that it is so easy to get lost in the shuffle of many things and lose sight of the main thing. The whole idea of seeking first the Kingdom of God and my righteousness has pretty much been upstaged by "be here, do that, hurry on to the next thing," and very little time being still to seek and know that I am God. The next twenty years will accelerate at a very risky speed.*

Lesson 11: The hurried scramble of this age makes it even more important to let God order our days.

I sensed the Lord saying: *Because time is advancing so rapidly, even little mistakes, dropped balls; and forgotten duties can have devastating consequences. There has never been a time when it has been more important to let ME order your day.*

I always tried to let God order my days but I sensed I

needed to let God give order to each part of each day.

He said, *"Part of ordering your day is asking me to give order to each day. This is best done in the evening, but can be done in the morning too. Just ask me to show you what is most important for each segment of each day: morning; afternoon; evening and night. When you do even one or two of My most important assignments during a few of these periods, you will see great shifts occur and your work will actually become easier, less stressful and more productive--whether your work is watching infant children, running a business, taking care of the sick or ministering in the Kingdom.*

Lesson 12: We can't run on yesterday's steam or anointing.

I was led to a familiar passage.

> I am the true vine, and my Father is the gardener. He cuts off every branch in me that bears no fruit, while every branch that does bear fruit he prunes so that it will be even more fruitful. You are already clean because of the word I have spoken to you. ⁴ Remain in me, as I also remain in you. No branch can bear fruit by itself; it must remain in the vine. Neither can you bear fruit unless you remain in me. "I am the vine; you are the branches. If you remain in me and I in you, you will bear much fruit; apart from me you can do nothing. John 15:1-5.

God said, *"I have used your failure to bring a power cord for your computer to teach you things that you probably would have overlooked. There remains the most important lesson: many Christians try to run on temporary or back up battery power--and they can for a short season. They can run in their own human strength for a while or even draw from earlier deposits from treasures stored within. But doing so is temporary at best, and soon the drawn down of power becomes so great that anointing is lost.*

It is far better to stay connected to the main source of power. I have told you of late that I call you to be my vessel or channel, so my love, grace, mercy, salvation, healing, deliverance and provision can flow through you. When you are my vessel you do not rely on what has been stored up or even that which is temporary. Instead you find the eternal strength to do what you are called to do. At that point I am the vine and you are the branch that bears much fruit to my Father's glory.

Chapter 18
Overcoming Obstacles to Healing

God's original design for people did not include sickness or death. Such things are part of the curse and certainly more Satan's work than God's.

The speakers I had lined up for one of our Kingdom Advance meetings canceled without much notice. I groaned and cried out, "Oh God, now what?" and left it in God's hands. The next morning Pam and I sat down for our devotions and the Lord began to speak about overcoming obstacles to healing. I sensed I was to wait, listen, receive, write and share this revelation.

During my first 15 years of ministry I had a traditional evangelical approach to healing that left a lot of room for unanswered prayer. We saw a few people we prayed for healed--but not usually until after they went to the doctor. We anointed the sick but without much anointing. There were very few instant healings and no miracles.

Then the Holy Spirit started bursting my old wineskins and developing new ones to hold new wine--and people began to be healed regularly.

There were not many miracles where the blind see or the lame walk, but many healings of backs, arthritis, headaches, colds, sinus problems and the like. We also learned to fight sickness--and quit having the flu every year like we used to before 1995.

But even after people began to receive healings I

thought, "Lord, if it is your will, please heal, but none the less--not my will, but thine be done." Such thinking wrongly assumes that it is God's will that people be miserable. Will there be sickness in heaven? Of course not! So when we pray "thy Kingdom come, thy will be done, on earth as it in heaven," that doesn't leave room for sickness. The Bible says that death is the last enemy to be overcome, not illness.

Are we right to assume that when healing does not come that it is God's will that the person remain sick? Could it be that there are personal or generational obstacles to healing that must first be overcome? Is it possible that we have an enemy that wants to kill, steal health and destroy well-being?

People ask "Why me?" but they don't ask God and wait for an answer. When healing doesn't come we should ask the Lord why, and wait for His answer. What hinders the healing we seek?

Few people have the gift of miracles. That is why we are amazed when we hear of the lame walking, the blind seeing and creative miracles of new eyes or new limbs forming. There is a difference between the anointing for miracles which move beyond human imagination, and healings which should be common in every Church. As we focus on healing from things like cancer, arthritis, respiratory problems, and the like we need to ask, "What hinders divine healing?"

The Strongest Schematic and Greatest Obstacle to Healing Seems to be Un-forgiveness.

Ephesians 4:26-27 says that unforgiveness gives the devil a literal foothold in our lives. In Matthew 18:24-35 Jesus told the parable of the King and his servants--including the one that had been forgiven a great debt but who would not forgive another a much lesser debt. Jesus concluded that the unforgiving person would be turned over to the tormentors.

> Then his lord, after that he had called him, said unto him, O thou wicked servant, I forgave thee all that debt, because thou desiredst me: Shouldest not thou also have had compassion on thy fellowservant, even as I had pity on thee? And his lord was wroth, and delivered him to the tormentors, till he should pay all that was due unto him. So likewise shall my heavenly Father do also unto you, if ye from your hearts forgive not every one his brother their trespasses. Matthew 18:32-35 KJV.

Some of those tormentors include painful and crippling diseases. When there seems to be an obstacle to healing the first question to ask is "Is there someone you need to forgive?" Lack of forgiveness seems to be the major obstacle to healing.

In my early days of healing and deliverance ministry I was ministering in Flint, Michigan. After teaching a divine healing seminar, we held a healing service. I will never forget the lesson I learned about unforgiveness and torment that night.

A dear old saint came forward for prayer concerning crippling arthritis pain. Her greatest pain was in her right shoulder and she could barely lift her arm. I asked her to show just how high she could lift it, and with grimaces of pain she lifted it to just above her waist.

I prayed the prayer of faith and asked her to try her arm again but there was no improvement. So I invited some Elders to join us in prayer as we prayed the prayer of faith again, and anointed her with oil. Again I asked her to lift her arm and again there was no improvement. Feeling desperate I asked God what was going on and he said, "She needs to forgive." I asked the lady, "Who do you need to forgive?"

She replied, "I will never forgive her!" So I asked, "Who won't you forgive and for what?" She said, "My mother, because she had to have known what my step-father was doing to me." This woman was so old that she had been married to the same man for over fifty years. She loved the Lord, was faithful to her church and everyone liked her. Her mother had died years before.

I asked her if arthritis was a tormenter to her. And she exclaimed, "Oh yes, I am constantly tormented by it." I took her to the parable of the man whose debt was forgiven who would not forgive his offender. I explained how he was handed over to the tormenters, and suggested she might have been handed over to the torment of arthritis because of her unwillingness to forgive her mother for not protecting her.

Her mother had done a horrible thing to her. Rather than protecting her daughter from the insidious sin of her stepfather, she looked away. I explained that vengeance is the Lord's and He will repay, but judgment is God's responsibility and not ours.

After the woman understood the link between unforgiveness and torment she chose to forgive her mother. We had spent so much time talking that I had forgotten exactly how high the woman could lift her arm, so I asked her to try again.

She lifted her hand way over her head and began to weep while exclaiming, "I am healed, I am healed!" I thought, "Wow, this woman's healing had been hindered for decades through unforgiveness."

Please understand the link between unforgiveness and torment. Jesus taught about this link. There are other ways to deal with torment, but one necessary way is to agree with God's blueprint for your life that includes forgiving all who have hurt you.

In our seminars I illustrate this by having a large man grab my arm and hold on to it. I say, "Pretend I hurt this man and he doesn't forgive me". I go on to show how what I did controls the man even if I am unaware of how I hurt him. Then I move on to the clincher by saying that any demon that I may have, has legal access to move through me and into the man until he chooses to forgive me and let go.

Vows and Oaths are Another Hindrance to Healing.

Another schematic and hindrance to healing is oaths and vows especially, those made in secret societies like the Masonic Lodge, Eastern Star, Pythian, Shriners and the like. Even pledges made in sororities or fraternities can hinder healing. The Hippocratic Oath can also bring problems. A female doctor who is part of the International Society of Deliverance Ministers shared her testimony of how she had to renounce the Hippocratic Oath she had made to achieve victory over a specific problem.

Whenever there is a hindrance to healing or deliverance I always check first to see if there is unforgiveness. If there isn't, I check to see if there was any personal or generational involvement with the Masonic Lodge or Eastern Star.

Jesus told us to let our yes be yes and our no, no for anything more than that is of the evil one. (Matthew 5:37) Secret societies that require oaths and vows violate the Word of God.

James implies that oaths and vows lead to condemnation!

> Above all, my brothers, do not swear--not by heaven or by earth or by anything else. Let your "Yes" be yes, and your "No," no, or you will be condemned. James 5:12.

Many professional deliverance ministers who are members of the International Society of Deliverance Ministers make the Masonic Release Prayer a prerequisite to a deep healing and deliverance appointment. Some people think they are safe because they don't think their parents belonged to the Masonic Lodge, but the Bible is clear: generational sins and curses can be passed down to the third and fourth generation.

Most people cannot name their ancestors four generations back, let alone tell whether they made oaths or vows contrary to the Word of God.

Let me share part of a testimony from a dear woman in our church who went through a Masonic Release from **www.jubileeresources.org.**

> My dad was a lifetime member of a Masonic Lodge. He was a 32nd degree Mason. He had all the memorabilia and I never gave it a second thought of why he belonged to that lodge any more than I gave any thought of him being a member of other organizations. A few years ago through Apostle Carr I started hearing different things about the evil which is connected to the Masonic Lodge. He had been trying to get me to go through the Masonic deliverance to confess and renounce it from my family line. I resisted for quite a while because I didn't think it was necessary.
>
> Then one day I experienced some of the worst pain in my back. It was a sharp stabbing pain that went down my buttocks into my leg causing me to have problems walking, sitting and even sleeping. Every morning I would have to sit on the edge of the bed before I could put my feet on the floor, because if I stepped the wrong way the pain would shoot down my

leg so bad I would almost lose my balance. This went on for a while and I had the church pray for me, anoint me, do the "leg out" command. It seemed to help a little bit, but in a few days it was right back again.

Apostle Carr said it was time for me to go through the Masonic deliverance. I was amazed at the things that I read, confessed, and renounced to break this curse on my family. There were two things that were specific that really caused me great concern. Men who go through the ritual have to be hooded, and they say weird vows. It was hard for me to see in my own mind my dad doing this.

But then it talked about the control of the mind, and how it affects the mind. My dad had Alzheimer's to the point where he couldn't call his children by name, he couldn't link which kids belonged to what son or daughter, he couldn't remember how to do anything he enjoyed, like cooking, and he couldn't remember how to do anything from the business he had for 70 years.

I was blown away by this and began weeping because as I realized it was the Masonic oath that had contributed to his Alzheimer's. It may not have been the total cause, but I knew it affected it when I read how it affects the mind. Then it talked about the hearing. Again, I was blown away, because later in life my dad had to have a hearing aid in both ears to hear anything.

After a couple of hours of exhausting reading, confessing and renouncing I came against the pain in my back and sciatic nerve. Once I renounced all of that Masonic mess and received healing and deliverance, the nerve released and the pain was gone just that quick.

I still have some arthritis and stiffness, but the nerve pain has never returned and I am so thankful. I know that any oath a person has to take in secret and not tell anyone about it, cannot be good. ~LB

Generational Curses and Iniquities are an Obstacle to Healing.

When disease follows an ancestral line there may be a curse that needs to be broken. If it is hereditary it may be that the punishment for the generational sins of the fathers is being passed down to the third and fourth generation. In that case the sins of the forefathers (and mothers) should be confessed like Daniel and Nehemiah did.

For example, African Americans are particularly susceptible to sickle cell anemia. I met with a precious mother of an 11 year old son who had been tormented with the pain of sickle cell for several months. One of his sisters also has that disease in her DNA. God immediately took us back to the curse of Noah against Cain and his descendants. We broke that curse and I've heard second hand that his condition has improved considerably since then. I spent a whole month studying how Noah's curse against Cain played out in his descendants and it went far beyond the third and fourth generation. I hope to put this into a small book in the near future.

Some think that Christians cannot suffer the effects of generational curses. They are welcome to their opinion but I have never heard anyone that walks in healing or deliverance agree with that. Jesus died so every person can be saved but not all appropriate his blood for salvation.

Jesus also died so every person can be healed but not all appropriate his blood for healing. Jesus died so every person can be released from curses but not all appropriate his blood against personal and ancestral curses.

**Word Curses are a Powerful Schematic
and hindrance to Healing.**

I used to work with a man who was susceptible to word curses. We could say, "Bob, you look a little pale, you must be getting sick," and within a few hours he would come into agreement with our words and go home sick.

Doctors are paid to find out what ails us and to report their findings. The problem comes when the patient comes into agreement with the hopelessness of medical diagnoses. It is far better to agree with the Word of God that says "by his stripes we were healed."

My father had heart problems and many open heart surgeries, by-passes and the like. He always thought that I carried too big a load and worked too hard and he said things like "You will have a heart attack by the time you are 50." I immediately renounced those words because there was power in them to kill. By the way, 50 seems young to me now and I haven't had heart problems. Charles Capps wonderfully presents the power of the words we confess in his little book "God's Creative Power for Healing."

When people start speaking about how old they are getting or how their bodies are breaking down, the devil is happy to empower those words to hold them in bondage to illness or accelerated aging. We must be careful of our words because they have power to quicken or to kill.

⸰ The power of life and death are in the tongue.
Proverbs 18:21.

**Not Being Dedicated to the Lord or Baptized,
can be a Schematic and Obstacle to Healing.**

Doris Wagner oversaw the department of deliverance for WLI when I was doing my graduate work. She has tracked how much easier deliverance and healing comes in people who were baptized or dedicated to the Lord as infants. While I prefer dedication of children over infant baptism, I believe that which is dedicated to the Lord has special protection from the Lord.

But what about people whose ancestors dedicated them to Japanese, Chinese, Native American or other cultural gods? Such dedications often include a curse of destruction for anyone who breaks allegiance with these gods of other nations. These dedications bring obstacles to healing that can be overcome.

Demonic Invasion is an Obstacle and Schematic that Hinders Healing.

One third of the healings in Mark include deliverance. The Gospels show that three out of ten of Jesus' healings involve rebuking demons. Time and again Jesus said things like "you deaf and mute spirit," or "spirit of infirmity," when he was healing the sick.

A spirit of death can come upon an unborn child through the death wish of a parent or grandparent. Bronchial asthma is often linked to such a death wish. High fevers are often linked to a spirit of infirmity. With children we often have a child's temperature taken, pray and rebuke the spirit of infirmity and see an immediate drop in fever from 102 - 104 to normal!

Unbelief is a Huge Obstacle to Healing.

Faith usually needs to be present for healing to be released. It can be the faith of the one praying, the faith of the one being prayed for or the faith of the one who brought the sick person to be healed. I think it was the faith of the men who lowered the man through the roof that brought healing to the invalid man.

Years ago I wouldn't minister deliverance to people unless their pastor was in agreement. There was a family in a nearby town who wanted me to minister to their mother. Her pastor disagreed, saying the woman didn't need deliverance, but just needed to be more faithful to the church, and to Bible reading, prayer, and tithing. So I refused to minister. She grew worse and was put in a Psych Unit for advanced Alzheimer's.

I was becoming familiar with Alzheimer's. My father married my wife's mother a few weeks before Pam and I married. About fifteen years later we built an addition and moved my father and mother-in-law into our home so we could watch over them as they grew older. Pam's mother had begun to show signs of dementia and within a few years she had full blown Alzheimer's. We prayed and saw miraculous healing when she had a stroke and later when she had a heart attack, but we never saw her healed of Alzheimer's.

About that time I was doing a seminar in Coldwater, Michigan and a woman was brought from a Psych Unit for healing of Alzheimer's. I had great compassion, but little faith, but they insisted that I pray concerning her disease.

So I laid hands on her, rebuked Alzheimer's, and watched and prayed over her while she was slain in the Spirit. A few minutes later she sat up and her Alzheimer's was gone! That had nothing to do with my faith but everything to do with the faith of her family. Later I discovered this was the same woman whose pastor said all she needed to do is be more faithful. Since then, I no longer require a person's pastor's approval before I work deliverance or inner healing-- there are far too many ministers who do not understand the need of deliverance.

Passivity is a Huge Schematic and Obstacle to Healing.

The devil will do anything to kill, steal, and destroy that he is allowed to do. When people sit back and accept a condition or diagnosis with no resistance, the devil has the upper hand.

Aside from direct spiritual warfare there is a cry that God hears. When the Israelites became so miserable that they started to cry out to God, He heard their prayer and raised up the Prophet Moses to lead them to freedom.

In Luke 18 Jesus finishes the parable of the unjust judge by saying, "And will not God bring about justice for his chosen ones, who cry out to him day and night?" The word "cry" is found in 160 Scriptures and "cry out" in 71.

In Mark 10 a blind man, Bartimaeus, was sitting by the roadside begging.

> When he heard that it was Jesus of Nazareth, he began to shout, "Jesus, Son of David, have mercy on me!" *Many rebuked him and told him to be quiet, but he shouted all the more,* "Son of David, have mercy on me!"
> Mark 10:47-48. (emphasis mine)

This man was passionate in his prayer. Barbara Yoder wrote the book <u>The Cry That God Hears</u>, which explains this concept in detail. The point is, there are times when the passion of God's response reflects the passion of our request.

A mother in a supermarket or playground can hear her child's cry above all the noise. Our Heavenly Father hears those who cry out to Him for healing.

Deception is a Familiar Obstacle to Healing.

As a deliverance minister I continually see how the devil's scheme of deception hinders people from pressing into

God for divine healing.

The devil is as active in modern health care as he was in medicine men and psychic healers.

Michael Elmore wrote the book, <u>The Occult Invasion of Health Care</u>. It is an eye-opener about how the occult has even entered main stream nursing care through Theosophy, Reiki, Therapeutic Touch, Healing Touch and other deceptive or counterfeit treatments.

Even Christians fall for the devil's tricks thinking "If it works, it must be of God." We need to remember that the Egyptian magicians replicated many of Moses' miracles. Hinduism and Buddhism are at the root of many alternative treatments including Palmer Chiropractic, Acupuncture, Healing Touch (not to be confused with the laying on of hands by the Elders) and the like. Believers are spending their resources on all sorts of treatments; Iridology, Chelation therapies, and the like, without ever asking God or their ministry leaders how they feel about such practices. Consider how God feels about such things.

> Why then have these people turned away? Why does Jerusalem always turn away? They cling to deceit; they refuse to return. 6 I have listened attentively, but they do not say what is right. No one repents of his wickedness, saying, "What have I done?" Each pursues his own course like a horse charging into battle. 7 Even the stork in the sky knows her appointed seasons, and the dove, the swift and the thrush observe the time of their migration. *But my people do not know the requirements of the LORD.*
> Jeremiah 8:5-7. (emphasis mine)

Disobedience is one of Satan's Favored Obstacles to Healing.

There is a ministry in Novi which invited me to come

once a month to do a couple of days of back to back deep healing appointments. One woman came who was raised Catholic and is now a member of a Presbyterian Church.

She is a young career woman but plagued with physical problems-- the worst of which was Candida. I asked her what she had tried for relief. She had gone to a Native American Sweat Lodge, Native healers, tried Yoga, Reiki, Chiropractic, and several other alternative treatments.

I asked if she had ever asked the Elders of her Church to pray a prayer of faith over her and anoint her with oil like the Bible tells us to in James 5:14-16. That thought had never crossed her mind. Then as she thought about it, she didn't know if the Elders in her church would anoint her if she did ask. I hope she tries--and I hope she will find a different church if they refuse to anoint her and pray for her.

Jesus paid the price for our healing, but we have the responsibility for dealing with every hindrance and obstacle to healing so we can walk in divine health.

Chapter 19
God's Blessings Come From Doing God's Will God's Way

God's schematic is that we obey him and enjoy the blessings of divine health. It is time to overcome obstacles to healing. In this chapter I will share what I believe to be a simplified version of God's plan to transform us from illness to health. We will visit each schematic and obstacle from the last chapter with God's antidote.

Unforgiveness

We ask people to bow their heads, close their eyes and form a cup out of their hands. Then we ask the Holy Spirit to bring to their minds the people they need to forgive. One at a time we lead them into purposeful forgiveness as they place the offenses they suffered in that cup. When they are all done we ask them to visualize giving that cup to the Lord. Then we discuss what they sense him doing with it. When they have forgiven all they need to forgive, we ask them if they are willing to ask God to forgive the people that have hurt them too. If they are unwilling, they may still need to work on forgiving.

It is helpful to have them forgive while remembering how they felt when they were hurt. If they were hurt at age ten, I may ask the "ten year old within them" to do the forgiving. Once their forgiveness is complete we ask the Lord to pull every root of bitterness from them. Then we cast out the spirits of bitterness.

Oaths and Vows

We lead people in confessing the sins of their ancestors, including all known or revealed oaths and vows. We encourage them to forgive their ancestors for the problems such oaths and vows have brought into their lives. Then we help them renounce them and ask God to break the power of such vows. We often lead them through a Masonic Release as well.

Generational Curses and Sins

We help people confess the iniquities of their father and his generational line, especially sins which led to curses or iniquitous patterns. We then have them do the same with the sins of their mother and her generational line. We then help them confess wherever they have come into agreement with ancestral sin. Finally, they renounce them and ask God to break the power of such vows.

Word Curses

The first step is forgiving those who have cursed you. Then it is important to confess any negative confessions you have made. Confess where you have come into wrong agreement with Satan or hurtful words and purposely renounce such word curses and break their power.

Dedications

If possible, learn as much you can about the dedication that was made so you can be thorough in renouncing it. Confess sins of ancestors, especially dedication to Native American or foreign gods. I even suggest that people confess and renounce infant baptism. Once confession is made it is time to renounce them and ask God to break the power of such dedications.

Unbelief

Forgive those who have taught you that God doesn't speak or heal today. Confess all unbelief. Exclaim: "I do believe; help me overcome my unbelief." Then renounce unbelief and command any spirits of unbelief or doubt to leave.

Passivity

Confess and renounce all passivity and apathy. Cry out to the Lord until he releases his zeal to you.

Deception

Confess where you have turned away from the Lord to deceptive ways that have not brought healing or peace to your souls. Renounce alternative treatments as the Holy Spirit brings them to mind and command spirits that took advantage of those things to leave.

Disobedience

Confess and repent of turning away from the Lord and not following His instruction to call for the elders when you have been ill.

This may seem like a lot of work but it is worth it. It is better to spend the time removing obstacles to healing than to go through weeks and months of medical tests trying to find out what is ailing you.

God not only wants to heal today but He wants us to live in divine health. Our part in that is removing obstacles.

Chapter 20
Stumble Through Da' Clutter or
Stand Up and De Clutter?

We saw from Genesis 1 that Satan brings chaos but God likes to step into chaos and speak order. Preachers used to say "Our brains are like computers-garbage in and garbage out." I used that many times to warn people about what they were feeding their minds. But things have changed and it is increasingly difficult to control everything that bombards our thinking. There is negative thinking and negative people just about everywhere we go.

Television, radio, work or school all release garbage that comes in and attaches until we purposely remove it. Today the computer illustration isn't a simple matter of garbage in--garbage out. Instead there are viruses, spyware, malware, pop up ads and a host of other things that worm their way into our computers and slow them down. I've had computers actually freeze up because of outer chaos. The same can happen in our lives and homes.

Just as good and bad junk can clog up computers so they slow down or go into hibernation to avoid crashing, so can good and bad clutter clog up our lives to where we become so slow that we may crash or hibernate. Much of what we call "burn out" has little to do with how much there is to do, but everything to do with the amount of clutter that must be defragged if we are going to move forward in this world.

    A motivational speaker said each undone task we have left to do takes up a synapse in our brain, and it keeps us from using that synapse for more pressing concerns. That, in turn, leads us to feel like we can't get anything done. He used the example of a stereo in his garage which only partially worked, and which would probably never get fixed. It was taking up valuable shelf space as well as using up his brainpower, preventing him from a more useful life purpose.

    Therefore I ask, are you going to keep on stumbling through Da clutter or stand up and purposely De clutter your life and home? God directs us to de clutter.

> So then let's also run the race that is laid out in front of us, since we have such a great cloud of witnesses surrounding us. *Let's throw off any extra baggage,* get rid of the sin that trips us up, ² and fix our eyes on Jesus, faith's pioneer and perfecter. He endured the cross, ignoring the shame, for the sake of the joy that was laid out in front of him, and sat down at the right side of God's throne. Hebrews 12:1-2 CEB. (emphasis mine)

We Can Choose to De-clutter the Stuff

    In Luke 12 a man came to Jesus and asked him to arbitrate his inheritance with his brother. Jesus refused and gave them this warning:

> Then Jesus said to them, "Watch out! <u>Guard yourself</u> against all kinds of greed. After all, one's life isn't determined by one's possessions, even when someone is very wealthy." Then he told them a parable: "A certain rich man's land produced a bountiful crop. He said to himself, What will I do? I have no place to store my harvest! Then he thought, Here's what I'll do. I'll tear down my barns and build bigger ones. That's where I'll

store all my grain and goods. I'll say to myself, You have stored up plenty of goods, enough for several years. Take it easy! Eat, drink, and enjoy yourself. But God said to him, 'Fool, tonight you will die. Now who will get the things you have prepared for yourself?' This is the way it will be for those who hoard things for themselves and aren't rich toward God."
Luke 12:15-21. (emphasis mine)

Does anyone NOT have too much clutter in their home, car, nightstand, magazine rack, and office? I do! A year ago last summer my wife and I moved our bedroom into the room we built for our parents before they died. I still haven't finished sorting through the stuff in my old closet -- even though I've filled my new closet. I've learned that "meaning to do something about it doesn't get it done."

Last fall I read an article by a woman in a small church who determined, along with a small group from her church, to do something about the clutter in their lives and closets. They agreed to take one thing a day and put the clutter in a box to give to Salvation Army or Good Will. They chose to do it for 100 days and at the end of that cycle, many of them felt so good about what they had accomplished, they decided to continue for another month or two.

We can choose freedom from da-clutter by deciding to de-clutter. Today I challenge you: Set one thing aside each day, starting today for one month, to give away or put into a private garage sale or a corporate one for missions. Simply pick a starting place and get started.

We can choose to de-clutter our emotions

I still have two out of several copies of the little book <u>None of These Diseases</u>, written by Dr. S. I. McMillin. He takes the title from Deuteronomy 28 and proves what the Bible says from the standpoint of modern medicine. The chapters include: Upset Mind--Sick Body; It's Not What You Eat--It's What Eats You; The High Cost Of Getting Even, Love Or Perish, David And The Giant--Worry, And Arthritis From A Panther Scare.

The devil wants us to stumble around in da clutter of damaged emotions. How we deal with hurt emotions can cause more harm than the original injury. We know that Ephesians 4:26-27 tells us that ongoing anger gives the devil a literal foothold in our lives. Negative emotions are not demons--but they do provide openings for demons. Anger is not sin--but it becomes sin if it is not dealt with properly. Unforgiveness IS sin that allows the tormentors room to torment.

Some may feel like their emotions have been attacked in every way possible. They've been lied to and about. Faithful friends have hurt them. But we are not responsible for what people did to us; we are responsible to guard the attitudes of our hearts.

> Above all else, guard your heart, for everything
>   you do flows from it. Proverbs 4:23.

The Bible addresses negative emotions like: fear, anxiety, worry, panic and the like and gives insight of how to guard our hearts from such things. Unfortunately emotional health is a missing ingredient in Christian discipleship---but it is not missing in the Bible.

Dr. Charles Kraft teaches that demons are like rats-- they go to where the garbage is. That is why we minister deep healing as a part of deliverance ministry. We need to de-clutter our emotions of their deep wounds. Jesus came to heal the fragmented heart.

Take a look at Hebrews 12 from the New Life Version:
All these many people who have had faith in God are around us like a cloud. *Let us put everything out of our lives that keeps us from doing what we should.* Let us keep running in the race that God has planned for us. Let us keep looking to Jesus. Our faith comes from Him and He is the One Who makes it perfect. He did not give up when He had to suffer shame and die on a cross. He knew of the joy that would be His later. Now He is sitting at the right side of God. Hebrews 12:1-2 NLV. (emphasis mine)

The many people who are a cloud of witnesses include the ones from Hebrews 11 who were mistreated in several ways -- yet they were commended for their faith.

Consider which negative emotion most clutters your life. Put that emotion in a cup and give it to God. Ask him to help you start processing it and then ask him to replace it with a positive emotion: for anger, forgiveness; for worry, trust; for anxiety peace; etc.

A young man moved into our house for five months and carried some hyper emotions with him. My wife observed it and the next morning the Lord woke her up with the thought to have him inhale the peace and presence of the Lord then exhale stress, anxiety and the like. That little exercise worked so well that we've used it several times on others with good results.

We can choose to de-clutter our thoughts

The book of Proverbs states that how we think controls how we act. If Satan can control our thoughts he can control our lives. I received the following note in my email that illustrates what I am talking about.

Our thoughts can easily distract us from Jesus and his

purpose and destiny for our lives and homes.

Let's revisit Hebrews 12 from the Amplified Bible.

> Looking away [from all that will distract] to Jesus, Who is the Leader and the Source of our faith [giving the first incentive for our belief] and is also its Finisher [bringing it to maturity and perfection]. He, for the joy [of obtaining the prize] that was set before Him, endured the cross, despising and ignoring the shame, and is now seated at the right hand of the throne of God. Hebrews 12:1-2 AMP.

There are times when it seems impossible to shut our minds down. That can be caused by a spirit of necromancy but it usually happens when our thoughts take us captive rather than vice versa. When our thoughts take us captive we are held in hostage to the clutter of our thoughts. Sometimes we can't even identify the thoughts that are troubling us. I think that is why David prayed:

> Search me, O God, and know my heart; test me and know my anxious thoughts. See if there is any offensive way in me, and lead me in the way everlasting. Psalms 139:23-24.

God says we are responsible to take our thoughts captive.

> The weapons we fight with are not the weapons of the world. On the contrary, they have divine power to demolish strongholds. We demolish arguments and every pretension that sets itself up against the knowledge of God, and we take captive every thought to make it obedient to Christ. 2 Corinthians 10:4-5.

To begin de-cluttering your thoughts, ask God to reveal your anxious thoughts. Write them down and choose the most troubling one first. Determine to take your thoughts captive by counteracting them with appropriate verses.

We can choose to de-clutter our input

A few days before one Christmas Pam and I were driving in heavy traffic between stoplights and the lady behind me was having an animated discussion on her cell phone with one hand while smoking with the other. I'm not sure how she was driving and she made me nervous. There's never been an age when people have been connected with more people, or possibly less connected with those who matter most. Our lives are cluttered with phone calls, texts, emails, voice mails, advertisements, and people talking. Even worse--children are not being heard by their parents!

A pre-school teacher shared recently that only two children in her class knew how to use a pair of scissors. Most of them tried cutting using both hands. But all those incoming students were adept with i-Pads and i-Phones.

The Holy Spirit gave me a picture of God calling, someone answering but telling him "Sorry, I've got to put you on hold." Then I realized how true that really is. Modern technology is so good at riveting our attention that we actually miss God's still small voice, and ignore the voice of our spouses and children. Ringtones have cluttered our lives and we need help.

I appreciate all the ways we can stay connected but fear we are connecting at such a superficial level that we aren't really connecting at all. There's a world of difference between looking in someone's eyes and reading their text. I saw a commercial where a couple was cuddled on the couch watching a show. The wife received a text. It was her husband saying "you need to move a little--my arm is going to sleep."

Technology needs to be a tool and not a tether

It's OK to use voice mail . . . and to turn your cell

phones off . . . and to get on Facebook when God leads you to, rather than when you fear missing something. It is so much better to communicate with your loved ones face to face rather than by Facebook. It is important to listen to your children and spouse with your eyes and ears, and not shut them off when the phone rings.

Ask God to show you when technology is replacing sociology. Ask your loved ones to tell you when they feel slighted by phones or Facebook.

Let's revisit Hebrews 12 from the Message:

> You see what this means—all these pioneers who blazed the way, all these veterans cheering us on? *It means we'd better get on with it. Strip down, start running—and never quit! No extra spiritual fat, no parasitic sins.* Keep your eyes on Jesus, who both began and finished this race we're in. Study how he did it. Because he never lost sight of where he was headed—that exhilarating finish in and with God—he could put up with anything along the way: Cross, shame, whatever. And now he's there, in the place of honor, right alongside God. When you find yourselves flagging in your faith, go over that story again, item by item, that long litany of hostility he plowed through. That will shoot adrenaline into your souls!
> Hebrews 12:1-3 MSG. (emphasis mine)

We need to strip down our tech lives and really pay attention to those we love most. I suggest picking "blackout times" from technology--perhaps during meal times or when you have a chance to communicate with family members. Ask God and your loved ones to reveal whenever you ignore a live message for an electronic message.

Remember, phones may be the next best thing to being there --but being there -- <u>really being there</u> -- remains the very best thing.

We can choose to de-clutter our schedules

There are different ways to look at time. For years my schedule was master rather than my servant. I was proud of 70-80 hour weeks for the church. Now I wish I could buy back those precious moments I lost with my family. We are always somewhere doing something. There are 168 hours in a week, and if we work 50 and sleep 56 we still have 62 hours left every week. I know that; but I also know that if we don't let God take charge of our time that everybody else will, until it is so cluttered we don't know whether we are coming or going.

It is so easy to let important things overtake *most* important things. Jesus said "Seek <u>first</u> the Kingdom of God and His righteousness," but even Christian families spend less than 15 minutes a day together in the Word and prayer, compared to several hours a day watching television, sitting at the computer or fiddling with cell phones. Somehow, we need to de-clutter our schedules or at least prioritize them so we actually do what is most important to God and to us. I understand our Christian priorities to be:

1. God: Our personal relationship with him. How much time do we spend each day relating personally to the Lord?

2. Marriage: Our most important priority next to the Lord is the one we have committed to love and to honor until death us do part. Do our schedules honor that priority?

3. Family: Parents are responsible to see that their children are properly trained, disciplined, educated and the like. Thank God for good schools and good teachers, but when we get to heaven we won't be able to use the excuse "that was the teacher's job or the church's job." Parents will be judged

according to how well they've parented their children.
4. Church: We are part of a Body and each part is to do its work. I have never known a person to neglect church who has not fallen away from the Lord, have you?

5. Others: The Bible calls us to help widows and orphans, to feed the hungry, visit the sick and go to those who are in jail. The Great Commission is not an option.

Did you notice that work was not even listed? Even though our first five priorities are too often neglected, we can't treat work like we do most priorities. You can't be 50% faithful to work and keep your job. You can't go to work when you feel like it and stay home when you don't. God views work as a means to take care of marriage, family, church and others. Work is not to be an end in itself -- even though our work is usually part of our prophetic destinies.

So, are you using your 168 hours each week in a way that pleases God? 1 Corinthians 10:31 says "whether we eat or drink we are supposed to do everything to the glory of God."

Who is it that fills in the slots to your calendar? Does your calendar reflect God's highest priorities for your life? There are certain interruptions that we cannot avoid. I have spent mornings trying to write sermons and had 3-4 people drop in for visits, several phone calls, and emails that wanted attention. And that's OK because next to God, people are our highest priority. But at the end of the day, have we done what is most important to God or do we need to de-clutter?

Pam and I have not missed more than a day or two in reading our Bibles and praying together since we married. The only way we've been able to do that is to do it first thing in the morning even when I have to be at the church at 6:00 a.m. Wednesday and Sunday mornings, or leave early for an appointment in another city. Years ago I made the commitment that I wouldn't leave home or even take my shower before doing devotions. God is our most important priority. We are trying to seek first the Kingdom.

Can I share a secret? We don't need to do everything we are asked to do. It really is OK to say "NO!" Before I give a few last tips on de-cluttering schedules let's revisit our Hebrews 12 from the Common English Version.

> Such a large crowd of witnesses is all around us! *So we must get rid of everything that slows us down,* especially the sin that just won't let go. And *we must be determined to run the race that is ahead of us.* We must keep our eyes on Jesus, who leads us and makes our faith complete. He endured the shame of being nailed to a cross, because he knew that later on he would be glad he did. Now he is seated at the right side of God's throne! So keep your mind on Jesus, who put up with many insults from sinners.
> Then you won't get discouraged and give up.
> Hebrews 12:1-3. CEV. (emphasis mine)

Choose a starting time to daily look at your schedule for the following day. I do mine in the evening as part of my Daily Listening Room.

Steps to De-cluttering Schedules:

1. Calendar all your must do's and do them on time.
2. Include God's "to-do's" as part of your daily journaling and make them part of your daily to do lists.
3. Prioritize your daily list according to Christian priorities.
4. Start and stick with number 1 and keep at it until done. Then go to 2, etc. until finished.
5. When interrupted, deal with it, and then go back to

what you were doing before the interruption.

When the Holy Spirit hovers over dark places of chaos, He waits to move in to bring light and order as soon as the prophetic word is spoken. It is time to speak a prophetic word over your own life. You may begin with "you are going to move into God's timing, season and priorities for your life."

Let us choose to surrender to God's lead as we break off Satan's schematics of clutter and disorder. May we listen for the words He wants us to speak as we speak order into our past, present and future!

Chapter 21
Blessing or Curse -- All in a Four Letter Word

I begin this chapter with a despised four letter word. If we don't take this four letter word seriously we will never be able to advance the Kingdom of God personally, let alone advance the Kingdom of God in the world.

This word is offensive to our flesh. We don't like its use at home, work, school and we especially don't like it at church where many consider themselves as voluntary reserves rather than enlisted soldiers.

There are some "questionable words" that are only used in older versions like the King James. You don't read about people saddling their asses in the NIV. You can't find the phrase "pisseth against the wall" in modern translations. But this despised word appears in every translation I've researched. It is found in its root form in 161 verses in the NIV, and its extended form in at least 60 more verses. Therefore, this verb is found in 221 verses and its concept, next to faith, is probably the most honored response to the Kingdom of God found in the Scriptures. Close the book if you must, but I am going to spell this word now: o-b-e-y.

In the Old Testament obey is always translated from shaw-mah'. Its root is "hee-er-op-rep-ace" which means "as becomes holiness." It is further described as "befitting men, places, actions or sacred things to God."

Shaw-mah is translated: hear 785 times, hearken 196

times, and obey 81 times plus various other ways in the KJV. It means: "to hear, listen to, obey, to hear of or concerning, to have power to hear, to consent, agree, and the like."

In the Old Testament these words describe how people are to listen to God, perceive what He says, and follow through by doing what He says.

In the NT, "obey" comes from a few different words. I am going to use the principle of first mention for each of these words. The principle of first mention takes the first time something is mentioned in Scripture (whether the entire Canon or in the Old or New Testament). The principle of first mention used the first mention of a word as a foundation and parameter for later references with the same word. In the pages that will follow I will take the first mention of Greek words that are translated obey and briefly expound them.

> The men were amazed and asked, "What kind of man is this? Even the winds and the waves obey him!"
> Matthew 8:27.

This "obey" comes from the roots: "hupo which means: by, under": and "ak-oo'-o which means to hear and hearken."

Some of its definitions include: "to be endowed with the faculty of hearing," "to attend to, consider what is or has been said," "to understand, and perceive the sense of what is said," "to give ear to a teaching or a teacher," "to comprehend, to understand."

Such obedience flows through hearing and understanding that Jesus is in charge, that we are to be under his rule, and that we must carefully listen to understand what the Master's orders are.

I have a beautiful, long haired retriever named Sarge. He has the most submissive heart I've ever seen in a dog. He wants to please. At the same time he is easily distracted by things that catch his attention. He loves to chase balls and retrieve them, and one day he taught me a great lesson on obedience as we were playing.

I was training him to stay until I gave him the command to fetch. I threw the ball and held my hand up indicating he was to stay where he was. As long as he kept his eyes on me he was OK. But when his eyes would wander to where the ball was he would start to wiggle and inch forward. But if I repeated the command he would put his eyes back on me and stay until I commanded him to fetch.

Sarge has a better grip on submission and obedience than most Christians do. All he has to do is keep his eyes on his master, and his desire to please overrides his temptation to run on his own. Let's move on to another Greek word for obey.

> Peter and the other apostles replied: "We must obey God rather than men! Acts 5:29.

This "obey" is translated from "pi-tharkh-eh'-o" which means: "obey, hearken unto, obey a magistrate and to obey a ruler or a superior." Its primary root word is "Archo" which is translated "rule over or reign over." It means "to be chief, to lead and to rule."

This indicates that our obedience is first to God because all right authority comes from Him. Therefore any authority that is not in right alignment with God is antichrist authority. For example, if a man uses his authority to tell his wife to look at porn, his authority is antichrist and should not be obeyed because it is not in right alignment with God. This concept becomes complex at home, work, school or church where leaders, who should protect their followers, wrongly use their authority to fulfill their own carnal desires. Great damage is done by perpetrators that use their authority for selfish desires. They victimize people in various ways and their victims often feel powerless to set boundaries because of the leader's position of authority. This leads to another Greek word translated obey.

> Obey your leaders and submit to their authority. They keep watch over you as men who must give an account. Obey them so that their work will be a joy, not a burden, for that would be of no advantage to you. Hebrews 13:17.

This word for obey (pi'-tho) is interesting because it includes the idea of trust of leadership and persuasion by leadership that leads to obedience. In the KJV it is translated "persuade 22 times, trust 8 times, obey 7 times, have confidence 6 times, believe 3 times" and" be confident twice". It means "to persuade, i.e. to induce one by words to believe, to make friends of, to win one's favor, gain one's good will, or to seek to win one, strive to please one."

Its definitions include, "to persuade unto, i.e. move or induce one to persuasion to do something, to listen to, obey, yield to, comply with," or "to trust, have confidence, be confident in."

Taking these amplifications for the words translated obey, we will now the word *obey* as an acrostic to further explain the good or bad schematics of obedience. All these things come to mind as we look at the "O" in obey in the following chapter.

Chapter 22 ~ O is Obey

In Matthew 21 the Pharisees tried to trick Jesus by asking "by whose authority" he was healing the sick. Rather than falling for their ruse he asked them in return, "John's baptism--where did it come from? Was it from heaven, or from men?" They resorted to situational ethics and couldn't come up with a politically correct answer so they said: "We don't know."

So Jesus began teaching a series of parables about the Kingdom that described the Kingdom of God in a way that Paul later summed up as:

⸸ For the kingdom of God is not a matter of talk
    but of power. 1 Corinthians 4:20.

Jesus began with a parable of two people -- one that said "You bet I will," but didn't, and the other that said "I won't," but did.

⸸ What do you think? There was a man who had two sons. He went to the first and said, `Son, go and work today in the vineyard.' "`I will not,' he answered, but later he changed his mind and went. "Then the father went to the other son and said the same thing. He answered, `I will, sir,' but he did not go. "Which of the two did what his father wanted?" "The first," they answered. Jesus said to them, "I tell you the truth, the tax collectors and the prostitutes are entering the kingdom of God ahead of you. Matthew 21:28-31.

We are so familiar with this parable I fear we don't realize how radical it is. If Jesus had been talking to President Barak Obama he would have said, "Barak, your secret service men who slept with and abused prostitutes and your own IRS agents are entering the kingdom of God before you."

I say this because Obama told the world on May 9, 2012 that he is in favor of same-sex marriage because his daughters can't understand why their friend's parents can't get married. Whether Obama is president or not, it is foolish to base policies and principles on what adolescent girls question, rather than on what the Word of God teaches!

But whether you get excited with or against me when I point out the president's arrogant pride that makes him think his opinion is weightier than the Word of God, let me assure you that I am not preaching to the president today. I am preaching to Christians who may or may not obey the Scriptures. Consider just a few, and contemplate how well you obey them.

⸱ Dear children, let us not love with words or tongue
but with actions and in truth. 1 John 3:18.

How well do your actions display your love?
⸱ Bear with each other and forgive whatever grievances
you may have against one another. Forgive as
the Lord forgave you. Colossians 3:13.

Unforgiveness and bitterness plague many believers and opens them to emotional and physical problems.
⸱ It is God's will that you should be sanctified: that you
should avoid sexual immorality; that each of you should
learn to control his own body in a way that is holy and
honorable, not in passionate lust like the heathen,

who do not know God. 1 Thessalonians 4:3-5.

Sexual immorality is prevalent even among Believers. A disturbing percentage of saints who come to me for deep healing and deliverance have had multiple sexual encounters outside of marriage *since* they were born again.

> Do your best to present yourself to God as one approved, a workman who does not need to be ashamed and who correctly handles the word of truth. 2 Timothy 2:15.

Too many Believers are biblically illiterate. I ask people how many of each kind of animal Moses took with him on the Ark. Few recognize at first that it was Noah that built the ark, not Moses. Even of those who do know it was Noah, not many remember he took but seven each of the clean animals.

The following excerpts come from the article "Bible Literacy Slipping, Experts Say," originally by Clayton Hardiman, Religion News Service.

> For comedians, there are subjects that are almost too easy--sure things that guarantee a laugh. For Jay Leno one late night, it was the Bible. During the taping of one of his television shows, Leno moved through his audience asking people what they knew about the Bible. "Name one of the Ten Commandments," he said.
>
> "God helps those who help themselves?" someone ventured. "Name one of the apostles," Leno told them. No one could.
>
> Finally, he asked them to name the Beatles. Without hesitation, the answer came ringing from throughout the crowd: George, Paul, John and Ringo.
>
> Leno wasn't spoofing the Bible that evening. He was spoofing our society, which claims grounding in Judeo-Christian principles and yet, according to a number of surveys, is increasingly losing touch with the scriptures

of those faiths.

Rev. Willie Burrel, pastor of Christ Temple Church in Muskegon Heights and a teacher with Western Michigan Bible Institute, also noted a decline in biblical literacy. "In order to be a Bible reader, you have to be a practicing Christian," he said. "There are a lot of *UN-PRACTICING* Christians."

The trend can be attributed in part at least to "the busyness of people's schedules," Burrel said. "Because of their work load and play load, people are spending less time in the **Word of God**."

> Avoid godless chatter, because those who indulge n it will become more and more ungodly. 2 Timothy 2:16.

It is great when Believers fellowship but there are times when I question whether their discussions have become godless chatter. If exclusion of any reference to God constitutes "godless chatter," then much of it is.

Years ago my wife and I were talking with Pastor Jack Eitelbuss, who was lamenting that so few people use the name Jesus. They may talk about God or the Lord but he didn't think they used Jesus' name very often. My wife commented "It's hard to call Jesus by his first name when you don't know him very well."

> Give and it will be given to you. A good measure, pressed down, shaken together and running over, will be poured into your lap. For with the measure you use, it will be measured to you. Luke 6:38.

I am blessed to be part of a very generous church but it wasn't always so. There used to be times that when special offerings were taken my wife and I gave 50 - 75% of the entire offering even though others had far more money. The fivefold office of apostles, prophets, evangelist, pastors and teachers has gained acceptance thanks, in part, to what C. Peter Wagner calls the Great Apostolic Reformation. But the only fivefold office that is usually funded well is the pastor of a local church. Give some thought to how generous you are in supporting the other apostolic offices.

⸹ Be devoted to one another in brotherly love. Honor one another above yourselves. Romans 12:10.

This command runs contrary to our dog eat dog culture. One area where we can examine our compliance to honoring others above ourselves is worship. How well do members of worship teams do with this?

⸹ Never be lacking in zeal, but keep your spiritual fervor, serving the Lord. Romans 12:11.

A bored student was quizzed "what does apathetic mean?" The boy answered, "I don't know and I don't care." If Jesus took the spiritual temperature of many Christians and churches I am afraid he would find them lukewarm.

⸹ Be joyful in hope, patient in affliction, faithful in prayer. Romans 12:12.

Muslims are instructed to pray five times each day, but some Christians seldom pray or only pray for a couple of minutes each day.

⸹ Share with God's people who are in need. Practice hospitality. Romans 12:11.

Has the church in our age released practical Christian charity to government entitlement programs? When is the last time you practiced hospitality or shared your personal resources with someone in need?

> You are under a curse--the whole nation of you--because you are robbing me. Bring the whole tithe into the storehouse, that there may be food in my house. Test me in this," says the LORD Almighty, "and see if I will not throw open the floodgates of heaven and pour out so much blessing that you will not have room enough for it. Malachi 3:10.

I run into lots of people who can't wait to have the curse of poverty broken off them. But they become angry or antsy when I suggest they may be under a curse because they refuse the Biblical principle of tithing.

We've considered a very small portion of Biblical commands that God gave so we might enjoy abundant life. One of the ways Satan schemes to kill, steal and destroy is by tempting us to ignore such commands. O is obey, B is blessing.

Chapter 23
B is Blessing

Blessing and favor always follow right obedience. Obedience is always rewarded while disobedience brings judgment. God clearly shared the link between obedience and blessing.

God shows the link between obedience and favor.

⸎ Now if you obey me fully and keep my covenant, then out of all nations you will be my treasured possession. Although the whole earth is mine, you will be for me a kingdom of priests and a holy nation.' These are the words you are to speak to the Israelites." Exodus 19:5-6.

He also shows the link between obedience, protection and victory.

⸎ Obey what I command you today. I will drive out before you the Amorites, Canaanites, Hittites, Perizzites, Hivites and Jebusites. Exodus 34:11.

Success is linked to obedience to God's Word.

⸎ Be strong and very courageous. Be careful to obey all the law my servant Moses gave you; do not turn from it to the right or to the left, that you may be successful wherever you go. Do not let this Book of the Law depart from your mouth; meditate on it day and night, so that you may be careful to do everything written in it. Then you will be prosperous and successful. Joshua 1:7-8.

When I entered Spring Arbor College four years after high school I wasn't a good student. High school was party time for me. I concentrated on my girlfriend, my job and having a good time and gave little thought to school work. Looking back I was a "submarine" student, often below "C" level. So when I started going to college I didn't do so well studying and taking tests. My grades were hovering below average even though I really was trying. I sought counsel from some of my favorite professors and they helped some, but not enough.

I finally turned to the Lord and he led me to the principle of meditating on the Bible which is found in Joshua 1 and Psalm 1. Both these passages promise success to those who mediate day and night on the Word, so I took God at His word and made Bible memory and meditation a high priority. I was amazed and grateful as my grades climbed so that I was actually on the Dean's list more often than not after I began meditating on God's word. My success was directly linked to my obedience.

Obedience leads to what I call "trickle down blessing." If people could see how obedience affects their descendants they would be quicker to obey. Deliverance ministers continually witness how the blessing of obedience and the curse of disobedience flow to the children and grandchildren. This principle is the underlying concept in Deuteronomy 28.

The first part of Deuteronomy 28 focuses on blessings that come through obedience.

> All these blessings will come upon you and accompany you if you obey the LORD your God: You will be blessed in the city and blessed in the country. The <u>fruit of your womb</u> will be blessed.... Deuteronomy 28:2-4a.
> (emphasis mine)

These blessings for those who obey and their descendants include blessings on or for:
- ☺ Financial increase.
- ☺ Travel.
- ☺ War and dealing with enemies both human and spiritual.
- ☺ Your property and community.
- ☺ You will be established.
- ☺ Non-Christians will fear and/or respect you.
- ☺ Prosperity.
- ☺ You will lend but not borrow.
- ☺ You will be the head and not the tail.
- ☺ Even the weather will favor you.
- ☺ The whole "sozo" salvation package that includes spiritual, physical, social and economic favor comes through obedience.
- ☺ Your blessing will flow to your children and succeeding generations.

The second part of Deuteronomy 28 links disobedience with a curse that is also passed down family lines. Derek Prince taught there are seven major indications of a curse passing down generational lines to the third and fourth generation:
- ☹ Mental and emotional breakdown
- ☹ Repeated or chronic illnesses (especially if hereditary)
- ☹ Bareness, a tendency to miscarry or related female problems
- ☹ Breakdown of marriage or family alienation
- ☹ Continuing financial insufficiency
- ☹ Being accident prone
- ☹ A history of suicides or unnatural or untimely deaths

(Quoted from <u>Blessing or Curse, You can Choose</u>, Derek Prince, Chosen Books, 2006 pg 53)

I now add three other indications of a curse to this list:
- ☹ Failure. Plans and projects meet with disaster.
- ☹ Life traumas; going from one crisis to another.
- ☹ Spiritually hindered in hearing God's voice, sensing His Presence, understanding God's Word, praying or using spiritual gifts.

O is obey, B is blessing, E stands for obedience in everything.

Chapter 24
E is in Everything

When I was a new Christian someone suggested "If Jesus is not Lord of your all, He is not your Lord at all." God's schematic for abundant living includes seeking first the Kingdom of God and His righteousness. Satan's schematic kicks in gear with the slightest acts or attitudes of rebellion.

Partial Obedience isn't enough.
Partial obedience is similar to partial faithfulness. No bride would be happy if her husband vowed 98% faithfulness. James said it this way:

> If you really keep the royal law found in Scripture, "Love your neighbor as yourself," you are doing right. But if you show favoritism, you sin and are convicted by the law as lawbreakers. For whoever keeps the whole law and yet stumbles at just one point is guilty of breaking all of it. For he who said, "Do not commit adultery," also said, "Do not murder." If you do not commit adultery but do commit murder, you have become a lawbreaker.
> James 2:8-11.

Christians who obey the Lord concerning church attendance, tithing, Bible reading and prayer, but who disobey concerning purity cannot expect favor or blessing from the Lord.

Delayed Obedience may lead to judgment.

In Numbers the people decided to obey God, but they did not obey when he first asked them, so their later "obedience" actually became disobedience.

> Early the next morning they went up toward the high hill country. "We have sinned," they said. "We will go up to the place the LORD promised." But Moses said, "Why are you disobeying the LORD's command? This will not succeed! Do not go up, because the LORD is not with you. You will be defeated by your enemies, for the Amalekites and Canaanites will face you there. Because you have turned away from the LORD, he will not be with you and you will fall by the sword." Nevertheless, in their presumption they went up toward the high hill country, though neither Moses nor the ark of the LORD's covenant moved from the camp. Then the Amalekites and Canaanites who lived in that hill country came down and attacked them and beat them down all the way to Hormah. Numbers 14:40-45.

There is a kairos or opportune season for every event under heaven. One sad example of this is when I was called by a desperate mother from another state concerning her son. He was a pleasant young man but his mother was concerned that he was going in the wrong direction. She saw my website and rightly discerned that he needed deep healing and deliverance. I agreed to meet with him when he visited his aunt who lives in my city. I mentioned that deep healing and deliverance only works for those that desire to be free. I met with the young man and offered to help him. I explained how we work deep healing and deliverance but he decided he didn't need help. He said "I'm OK" and left it at that. We prayed before I left and I asked the Lord to send help to him if and when recognized he needed help.

A few weeks later I received a sad text saying that he had been involved in a bizarre shooting and was dead. God tried to catch this precious young man's attention and he was offered deep healing. But his delayed obedience cost his life.

Doing the right thing the wrong way leads to judgment.

God wanted to release blessings back to the Israelites through moving the Ark back to Jerusalem. So the Ark was loaded up on a cart and they began moving it, fully assured they were doing God's will. But look what happened:

- When they came to the threshing floor of Kidon, Uzzah reached out his hand to steady the ark, because the oxen stumbled. The LORD's anger burned against Uzzah, and he struck him down because he had put his hand on the ark. So he died there before God. Then David was angry because the LORD's wrath had broken out against Uzzah, and to this day that place is called Perez Uzzah. David was afraid of God that day and asked, "How can I ever bring the ark of God to me?" 1 Chronicles 13:9-12.

David was mad when the Lord's anger broke out because of his disobedience. But he had tried to do God's will man's way. His anger should have been directed at himself, not God.

David had overlooked the command that the Ark was to be carried on poles, but ignorance of the law was no excuse. God judged the people for trying to do God's will, man's way.

Praise unto the Lord that he is willing to meet us when we cry out to him--even when we have brought our problems upon ourselves through disobedience. People may fail to connect their past disobedience with their present problems.

Couples that engaged in fornication or lived together before marriage seldom consider that they need to repent of past disobedience to enjoy present blessing. O is obey, B is blessing, E is in everything and Y is YOU.

Chapter 25
Y is You

One of the most amazing things about God's schematic is that each person is sovereign over his or her own life. You cannot make my decision to obey or disobey, and I cannot make yours. Parents teach their children obedience through love and discipline, but even the best parent cannot make a child always behave. Just think of how some of God's children behave!

The Bible tells people to obey their leaders, but I don't see anywhere the Bible tells leaders to force people to obey. During 39 years of ministry one of the saddest things I've witnessed is people who have lost their marriages, their homes, their jobs, their children, and their testimony simply because they would not listen, trust and obey their leader.

<u>True love empowers obedience.</u> The words love and obey are found together in both Testaments, but I will use what Jesus said.

> If you love me, you will obey what I command. Jesus replied, "If anyone loves me, he will obey my teaching. My Father will love him, and we will come to him and make our home with him. John 14:15, 23.

Jesus healed an invalid who laid on a mat near the Sheep Gate by a pool, which in Aramaic is called Bethesda. He had been there for 38 years, unable to work for a living, hoping for but not receiving his healing, because no one would move him into the pool when the waters were being disturbed by the angel. Jesus saw him, learned that he had been there a long time and healed him. But that isn't the end of his story.

> ⸗ At once the man was cured; he picked up his mat and walked. The day on which this took place was a Sabbath, and so the Jews said to the man who had been healed, "It is the Sabbath; the law forbids you to carry your mat." But he replied, "The man who made me well said to me, `Pick up your mat and walk.'" So they asked him, "Who is this fellow who told you to pick it up and walk?" The man who was healed had no idea who it was, for Jesus had slipped away into the crowd that was there. Later Jesus found him at the temple and said to him, "See, you are well again. *Stop sinning or something worse may happen to you.*"
> John 5:9-14. (emphasis mine)

Consider the following story of one woman's sin, Jesus forgiveness, and his warning.

> ⸗ And the scribes and Pharisees brought unto him a woman taken in adultery; and when they had set her in the midst, they say unto him, Master, this woman was taken in adultery, in the very act. Now Moses in the law commanded us, that such should be stoned: but what sayest thou? This they said, tempting him that they might have to accuse him. But Jesus stooped down, and with [his] finger wrote on the ground, [as though he heard them not]. So when they continued asking him, he lifted up himself, and said unto them, He that is without sin among you, let him first cast a stone at her. And again he stooped down, and wrote on the ground. And they which heard [it], being convicted by [their own] conscience, went out

one by one, beginning at the eldest, [even] unto the last: (they had finally learned to judge self rather than others) and Jesus was left alone, and the woman standing in the midst. When Jesus had lifted up himself, and saw none but the woman, he said unto her, Woman, where are those, thine accusers? Hath no man condemned thee? She said, No man, Lord. And Jesus said unto her, neither do I condemn thee: go, and sin no more. John 8:3-11 KJV.

I love preaching this story. I wonder where her male partner was and why he wasn't brought along. Jesus' actions show that mercy is far more redemptive than judgment. This woman wasn't free to go and sin no more until her condemnation was broken off. But there is something more that I want to point out.

I believe in grace and thank God for it, but grace is not a license to continue in sin. God will forgive any sin that is confessed, renounced and repented of. Jesus told the woman "Neither do I condemn you. Go and sin no more lest something worse happen to you!"

God's schematic for abundant living is realized through obedience. Satan's schematic to kill, steal, and destroy is activated through disobedience and the choice is ours. We can choose to obey and walk in favor or choose to disobey and reap Satan's schemes.

Conclusion

If you do a word search for "schemes" in the NIV Bible you will find it 18 times in the Old Testament and the following 2 times in the New Testament.

↳ In order that Satan might not outwit us. For we are not unaware of his schemes. 2nd Corinthians 2:10.

↳ Put on the full armor of God so that you can take your stand against the devil's schemes. Ephesians 6:11.

In Second Corinthians *schemes* is used in the context of forgiving and restoring a wayward brother. In Ephesians it is in the context of spiritual warfare. Both are important, but I conclude with another Scripture where a "strategy" (very similar in meaning to schematic) is used in ways that do not show up in a word search for the word "strategy":

↳ For though we walk in the flesh, we do not war after the flesh: (For the weapons of our warfare [are] not carnal, but mighty through God to the pulling down of strong holds); {through God: or, to God} casting down imaginations, and every high thing that exalteth itself against the knowledge of God, and bringing into captivity every thought to the obedience of Christ; {imaginations: or, reasonings} And having in a readiness to revenge all disobedience, when your obedience is fulfilled. 2 Corinthians 10:3-6 KJV (with publisher's notes in brackets)

Let me explain a few words from these verses that are

germane to schematics.

The word translated *war* is "strateuomai" and is translated war here, and warfare and soldier other places. It is defined as "to make a military expedition, to lead soldiers to war or to battle, (spoken of a commander); to do military duty, be on active service, be a soldier, and to fight." It is related to the word that we get *strategy* from.

The word translated *pulling down* is actually from the same root as casting down but in a different form here. It is the Greek word "kathairesis" which is translated "destruction" twice, and "pulling down" once. It means "a pulling down, destruction and/or demolition."

The word translated *strongholds* is "ochuroma" which means "to fortify, through the idea of holding safely." It is translated stronghold in the King James but can also be translated "a castle, stronghold, fortress, fastness, anything on which one relies, of the arguments and reasonings by which a disputant endeavors, or to fortify his opinion and defend it against his opponent".

The word translated *casting down* is "kathaireo" which is translated take down, destroy, put down, pull down, and cast down, in the King James. It is defined as "to take down, without the notion of violence: to detach from the cross one crucified, with the use of force: to throw down, cast down, to pull down, demolish, the subtle reasonings (of opponents) likened to a fortress, i.e. to refute, to destroy".

The concepts of the words translated "pulling down" and "casting down" include "being taken down with great violence, being utterly demolished or being impeached from office."

A key word that really stands out is the word translated *imaginations* in the King James or "arguments" in the NIV. It is the Greek word "logismos" that the English word "logic" comes from. It is translated "thought, imagination, arguments" and the like in different translations and verses. It means "a reasoning: such as is hostile to the Christian faith, a judgment, and decision: such as conscience passé."

The word translated *thought* in the King James is "noema," and is translated mind, device, and thought: It means "a mental perception or thought, an evil purpose" or "that which thinks, the mind, thoughts or purposes." It comes from the root which is translated "understand, perceive, consider or think" and means "to perceive with the mind, to understand, to have understanding" or "to think upon, heed, ponder, consider."

Proverbs 23:7a in the KJV, says "For as he thinketh in his heart, so [is] he."

If you take all these words and put them together you see the need of spiritual warfare to pull down, cast down, and impeach fortified reasonings of our logic systems and mental perceptions that come into agreement with Satan's schematics which lead to destruction and to take on the mind of Christ through being born of the Spirit, baptized in the Spirit, and continually filled with the Holy Spirit, so we will keep in step with the Spirit and flow according to God's schematic for our lives.

This is a choice that we all make intentionally or by default. God has given us personal sovereignty in the matter.

> And if it seem evil unto you to serve the LORD, **choose you this day whom ye will serve**; whether the gods which your fathers served that [were] on the other side of the flood, or the gods of the Amorites, in whose land ye dwell: **but as for me and my house, we will serve the LORD.** Joshua 24:15. (emphasis mine)

Endorsements for Schematics

> "...so that no advantage would be taken of us by Satan, for we are not ignorant of his schemes." 2 Corinthians 2:11

Too many believers are unaware of the schemes of the enemy. We know this to be true because each and every week in the Healing Rooms, we dress and bandage the wounds of the Body of Christ who come in to receive prayer for the hits the enemy has inflicted on them. Indeed, as Believers; we seem totally ignorant of the progressive revelation of the redemptive work of Christ through chronos time. Jesus Christ Himself is still anticipating the day when he will return as the Rider on the white horse whose name is Faithful and True and in a final act of thrilling victory; throw Satan and his minions into the fiery lake of burning sulfur for eternity. Until that day; we still have an enemy with which to contend; though his authority and length of days have been limited.

In this insightful book called *Schematics*, Dr. Douglas Carr unravels and reveals the age-old schemes that our arch-enemy; Satan, continues to wield against Christ's followers on the earth. As you read and apply these weapons of warfare described by Dr. Carr; you will find yourself winning battle after battle, and going from strength to strength in your warfare against Satan. Don't miss the gems in this book that will cause you to live as a victor until that day when we gather together for the wedding supper of the Lamb and proclaim Him, King of Kings and Lord of Lords!

--Beverly and Steve Bubb –
Michigan Healing Rooms State Directors

Doug Carr writes in this book about what I call faces; the faces of anger, of sin and bondage, the different faces of victory, and the face of God. This book not only explains the problems we face because of sin and its results, it goes on to explain how to move into continuous ongoing and unfolding victory. I know Douglas Carr. He exemplifies what he teaches and ministers with love and humility. This book is like a manual and will walk you through to victory and freedom and on into destiny.

Doug, Great job.

Barbara J Yoder
Senior Pastor and Lead Apostle
Shekinah Regional Apostolic Center
Breakthrough Apostolic Ministries Network
www.shekinahchurch.org
www.barbaraYODERblog.com

Made in the USA
Monee, IL
21 January 2023

25861988R00105